CLASSIFICATION: POETRY

A CIP catalogue record for this book is available from
the British Library.

Printed and bound in Great Britain.

*Cover photograph by courtesy of
the North West Tourist Board.*

This Scotland, Northern Ireland, Wales & East Anglia edition

ISBN 1-902803-80-9

First published in Great Britain in 2001 by
United Press Ltd
1 Yorke Street
Burnley
BB11 1HD
Tel: 01282 459533
Fax: 01282 412679
ISBN for complete set of volumes
1-902803-85-X
All Rights Reserved

© Copyright contributors 2001

www.upltd.co.uk

In the Eyes of
the Poet

Foreword

This book a significant milestone for all of us at
United Press. It is our first every summer
compilation of poems by different poets.
In the past, we have only produced a compilation
of this kind at the end of a year. But such is the
enthusiasm of poets who have already been
published with United Press, that we decided to
invite submissions for a summer compilation.
I'm very pleased to say that this project has been
so successful that we've already decided to repeat
it next year.

Within these pages you will find a wide variety of
material from poets of different styles and with
different ways of expressing themselves.
I never cease to be amazed by the variety of the
material that lands on my desk.
Working on this book has been entertaining,
interesting and even surprising. Now that it's
finished, I'm already looking forward to next year.

Peter Quinn, Editor

Contents

The poets who have contributed to this volume are listed below, along with the relevant page upon which their work can be found.

64	Suzi Batchelor	98	Carol Rees
65	Gary Finlay	99	Sandra Lowe
66	Robert John Moore	100	Roger Matthews
67	Norah Burnett		Lorraine West
68	Nicolas Byrne	101	Christopher Parks
69	Geraint Jenkins		Marian Curtis-Jones
70	Lynda Howell	102	Laura Fost
71	Martin Faulkner	103	Patricia Newton
	James Hinder	104	Marjory Price
72	Rebecca Punter	105	Tony Davis
	Glenys Moses	106	Rebecca Rees
73	Alwyn Jolley	107	Sonia B West
	Irene Morgans		Susan Revell
74	Dian Phillips	108	Patricia Titcomb
75	Christine Williams		Samantha Potts
76	Lorna Culshaw	109	Maxine Kaye
	Laura Neal	110	Karen Davies
77	Pamela Evans	111	Louis Don Barrow
	Lee Jones	112	Pamela Willison
78	Brydie McDonald	113	Dorothy Blakeman
	Sylvia Mudford	114	Grace Hubbard
79	Alan Wilson	115	Daphne Askew
80	Emma Owen	116	Gill Doyle
81	Glenys Broxton	117	Rebecca Hankins
82	Ann Briggs		Jean Regan
83	David Rosser	118	Joyce B Burton
84	Cheryl Phillips		Rebecca Glenn
85	Jean Adams	119	Jane Besser
86	Adrian Thomas	120	George Payne
87	Mal Phillips	121	Dave Stevens
88	Nina Froley	122	Becky Fowler
89	Julian Gaius Williams	123	Mark Rasdall
90	Joan Rees	124	Susan Cooper
91	Alwyn James		Alice M Reynolds
92	Lauren Evans	125	Cynthia King
	Valdo Funning	126	Candi Baxter
93	Valerie Thompson		Glenda Rowbottom
94	Karen Watkins	127	Alice Ackland
95	Meredith Vallis	128	Andrew Parker
	Gareth Wyn Davies		Diane Berthelot
96	Peter Arthur Butcher	129	Sylvia Davies
97	Primrose Matthews		Anna Whitley

130	David Fairchild
131	Henry William Mobbs
132	Chris Belcher
133	Muriel Roe
134	Victoria Ellen Painting
135	Sophie Johnson
	Belinda Allen
136	Janet Borrett
137	David Ross
	Megan Samuel
138	Christine Laverock
139	Suzy Boon
	Patricia Cox
140	Lizzy Usher
141	Peter Davey
142	James Allen
143	Bryony
	Aline Longman
144	Grahame Godsmark
145	Dennis Theobald
146	Sylvia Eden
147	Elizabeth Davies
148	Helen Persse
149	Sue Smith
150	Jackie Johnson
151	Caryn Squires
	Julie Ashton
152	Sarah Jondorf
153	Andrea Grimes
154	Sally Jane Barnes
155	Harold Stephenson
156	Peter Huggins
157	Andria J Cooke

KIND AND EVIL

The kind, gentle soul
innocently loves the evil one.
The kind, gentle soul
admires the evil one.
The evil one
ignores the kind gentle soul.
The evil one
hurts the kind gentle soul.
The kind, gentle soul
longs for the love of the evil one.
The evil one rarely gives it.

Sarah Lean, Quarter, South Lanarkshire

BATSI ON ANDROS

Like seagulls perching on a cliff
the white white houses line
the rock-hewn pier, and straggle drunkenly up the hillside
their red roofs piercing the deep blue sky.

In the early morning, not a sound is heard,
but the steady clip-clop of the donkey team
weighed down, not with saddle-bags
but refuse bins,
whose odour shames the air.

The waves rush up on the sandy beach
where the golden sand, sundried,
trickles through my fingers like the days and years.

Rena Livingston, Castle Douglas, Kirkcudbrightshire

*Dedicated to our granddaughter Soraya, who at eighteen
months old made our first holiday on Andros so memorable.*

THE BEHOLDER

In the eye of a child
Is discovery,
The world revealing itself
To daily wonder.

In the eye of a needle
Is awareness,
The sharpness matching
Thread and material.

In the eye of a storm
is the heart,
The core from which
All life force grows

In the eyes of the poet
Is something of each one
And more
He must be all things
To all people
As well as his own man.

Mary R Elliott, Edinburgh, Scotland

A SCOTTISH GRACE

Oh Lord, Wha blessed the loaves and fishes,
Please dae the same for this nicht's dishes,
And whether oor appetite's great or sma',
Mak' sure that there's enough for a'.
Amen

John Osborne, Edinburgh, Scotland

SECOND BEST

People talk of second best in a derogatory tone
But for me, my second best, well he is second best to none
He gave my life a meaning that it had lacked for twenty
years,
To my children he gave hope, a chance to brush away their
fears
The violence and power were gone, they now could be
themselves
To live their lives as they would wish, not as their father
wills
My children now are fully grown, all with children of their
own
He's granda to each one of them, and adores them every
one.
This caring, loving, gentle man, has patience by the score.
I need never search again for love, I couldn't ask for more.
I wouldn't change him for the world, he understands my
every need.
My second best, he takes first prize, in world, and thought,
and deed.

Frances Jaffray, Ellon, Aberdeenshire, Scotland

A GODLY BLESSING

Count your blessings every day,
Then sweep your troubles all away,
Your best blessing is God above,
Who is with you all the time with love.

Just lift your voice to God any time at all,
He is there to listen to your call,
Be it every day or night,
A prayer from you is his delight.

Samuel Jennings, Airdrie, Lanarkshire, Scotland

Born in Airdrie **Samuel Jennings** started writing poetry in 1990 when he retired. "My work is influence by my memories and the person I would most like to meet is Robert Burns because his poetry inspires me," said Samuel. He is aged 89 and is a widower with three children. Samuel has written over 50 poems and had most of them published. "Poetry is my chief hobby but my biggest fantasy is to manage the Scotland football team," he added. Samuel's biggest nightmare is to have his car stolen.

LONELINESS

My loneliness exists
In this empty home,
And it also sits
On me when I roam
The roads that I may seek
A presence, or a voice
That might in charity speak
A word, or give me choice
To be with them or not.

Fae Watson, Dounby, Orkney Islands, Scotland

GOD IS OUR HOPE

Yes You are our hope Lord
A bright shining light
To show us our way Lord
To know wrong from right

We go our own way Lord
Turn day into night
But You are our hope Lord
And You are our light

We are not without hope
You gave us Your Son
That good over evil
The fight can be won

Help us fight to do good
Have faith in Your Son
Our sins all forgiven
With hope for each one.

Mary Hudson, Argyll and Bute, Scotland

YOU CANNOT TOUCH THE SKY

You cannot touch the sky.
Just watch the clouds float by.

You might touch the moon.
Moonbeams can touch the sea.

You cannot touch the sun.
The sun can touch you.

You cannot touch a passing breeze.
You can touch a raindrop

You cannot touch a dream
Though you might touch the dreamer.

You cannot touch pain
But pain can touch you.

You cannot touch a babies cry,
But you can see and touch a babies smile.

You cannot touch time,
Only time can touch you.

You cannot touch a rainbow,
Or a memory.

You cannot touch the sky
And that will always be.

Christine Pond, Kirkbean, Dumfriesshire, Scotland

SPIRIT OF SPRING

Snowdrops are bursting through the ground,
For cheering the spirit they are profound,
Peeping through wintry earth, so pure and white,
They are the forerunners of spring.

Giving the impression that there is hope,
So despair not! The crocus and the daffodils will soon
Follow in the footsteps of the snowdrops,
Bringing a glorious colour to the Easter garden.

Gardening is a mystery, a living thing, an act of faith,
From small seeds and bulbs, personal pleasure they bring,
Who could imagine that in a season,
They would delight the eye without reason?

Annuals are joined by perennials, their splendour to show,
Side by side they grow, enhancing the shrubs,
Revealing the miracle of growth,
Which knows no bounds.

Contentment is a great asset,
Brought to life in each fact
Of growth and beauteous colour,
Lifting the spirit to an ethereal planet above.

Mary Lawson, Auchterarder, Scotland

UNTITLED

How I wish everyone could see..........
The glory of a November sunset........
The first snowdrop........
The beautiful rainbow after a heavy shower of rain......
The garden transformed from a weedy patch with the first
snow of winter........

A baby's toothless grin......
The Autumn leaves which fall as a golden shower
Oh how I wish everyone could see.

Vicky Wood, Aberdeen, Scotland

TIME OUT

Three decades ahead of egalitarianism-
enlightened ideology they call it:
vocationalism, with a past prescriptive
rhetoric of progressive and liberal doctrines.

The common denominator of ingrained awe
and respect curiously pervades eternal-
conditioned learning the pundits explain:
the response of the rod unspared, I fear/

Comparatives and superlatives clash and confront
as a measure of differentiation in the pedagogic
process of evolution and reform: change equals progress,
is the metaphor they dictate. There is no challenge.

Much appears in terms of deficit: would former
icons agree? it it doubtful.
Will the measure of efficiency in terms of waxed jargon
show threes decades into the millennium? We accept.

Frank Zwolinski, Dundee, Scotland

LOSS & BEREAVEMENT

Your name is often on my lips, increasingly silent so, not
wanting to hurt others.
Your face, your smiles are imprinted on the pictures in my
mind, but the essence that is you,lives on in my heart.
Silently and secretly we converse, and will do so until the
end of time. My ears will always hear you laugh. I find
myself looking with your humour at the world. The wonder
that was you will live on in me.

Patsy Boyd, Forfar, Angus, Scotland

SECRET

Am I with you tonight
Inside your head as you lie sleeping?

Do you touch my hair -
Golden burning fire
Covering my face
Hiding the truth
That smoulders in the ashes?

Do you feel my breath
Beneath your eyes?

Do you kiss my lips
As they whisper my dreams
To you?

Am I with you tonight?

I shall never know.

Michelle Melville, Fort William, Scotland

GIFT OF LIFE

The most precious gift a women could give
Is the chance to let a baby live
The pain you have will turn to joy
When you see your baby girl or boy

Imaging the look in a mothers eyes
It's a look of love, joy and surprise
And when your child gives you a first smile
You'll know that it's been all worthwhile

It isn't hard to be a good mum
Just give your child love, care and fun
A child is proof that dreams come true
And if you love them, they'll love you too

Although most of your freedom will be left behind
All you women bare in mind
That the most precious gift a women could give
Is the chance to let a baby live

Lisa Sweeney, Glasgow, Lanarkshire, Scotland

THE OLD SCOT'S BOTHY

A room in the attic with bare wooden floor
Plenty of bugs and fleas galore
A bed in a corner a chest in the middle
A pot neath the bed for the nightly piddle

Great in the summer when the day's works done
Open the skylight and let in the sun
But woe in the winter twas bitter at night
And a single gas mantle was the only light

An oil fired stove gave out little heat
A gas ring for cooking whate're was to eat
A cupboard for clothes a table and chair
No pictures to hang on walls that were bare

The blanket was threadbare the quilt was torn
But at least they were heavy so really quite warm
An alarm by the bedside to wake him each day
And dare he sleep in twould cost him some pay

Now the rural community has changed much of late
There's houses and cottages on every estate
The farm worker's life has reached sanity at last
Farewell to the bothy the scourge of the past

John Coull, Perth, Scotland

VISIONS OF YESTERDAY

Looking through the mists of time, first memories unfurl,
Playing with her favourite doll, a happy little girl.
Wrapped around with family love and sheltered from all
ills,
Starting out along life's path, the valleys and the hills

Then the school girl, neat and tidy, trying hard to please,
Growing, learning, having fun, the years roll by with ease.
(Strange, I often wonder, though I tried so hard - and yet
Never once throughout those years, was I a 'Teachers Pet'.)

Next came love and marriage, with a family to raise,
Caring, sharing, dreaming dreams, oh happy, happy days.
Looking backwards through the years, what wonders have
we seen
Microwaves and mobile phones, the television screen.

Dishwashers and videos, machines to wash the clothes,
What's next in line? what more can progress bring to us?
who knows!
We take so much for granted, but can forget so soon,
The greatest wonder of our time - WHEN MAN WALKED ON
THE MOON.

Elsie MacKenzie, Bishopbriggs, Scotland

NANCY

You went away and left me,
I know you couldn't stay.
Once again Im broken hearted.
So sad in every sort of way.
My constant companion, and my dearest
Friend for twenty years.
Is there any wonder when you died
I held you, and couldn't stop the tears?
"You were only a little cat", some might say,
But you brought me sunshine, fun and love
Into my life everyday.

Marion Henderson, Brechin, Angus, Scotland

TRUTH

I saw my hands today - but these were not my hands.
These hands were brown flecked - wrinkled - blue veined
with earth chipped finger nails.
Not my hands.
These were the hands of an old women.
I am not an old women.

I saw my face today - but this was not my face
This face was brown flecked - wrinkled - red veined
with weather beaten skin.
Not my face.
This was the face of an old woman.
I am not an old woman.

Mirrors can lie.
Cameras can lie.
But my eyes saw - Truth.

Dorrie Morrison, Stromness, Orkney Islands

CRANES

Standing silent and equally proud,
gazed at by a saddening crowd,
Their fate now in the hands of men, whom,
cannot see or would not care not of the doom,
destined for my sleepy town.

Guardians of the people looking out upon the Clyde,
they served their purpose, the industry now in slide,
unemployment sent to thousands of men,
one thing is certain,
you take them away,
You take away the heart,
of my sleepy town.

Kirsty Sandford, Port Glasgow, Inverclyde

CONQUEST OF TRADITIONS

An intense sense of wonder washes over me
I revel in your naivety
You squirm at my mirth, and across an expanse of longing
Our eyes lock, and all at once I know
My body explodes with wanton lust
My eyes become deep, deep pools, that draw you into their
depths
And the tendrils of lust, bond us together
In a tenuous, passionate moment
And you speak once more to me
The spell is fragmented, and I turn once more to reality
It's been a long evening, and just for a moment
I held you in my mind
And you?
You were possessed.

Cate Campbell, Aberdeen, Scotland

FASHIONABLE FLING

Unease and distrust appears prevalent today.
Respected principles in society have evaporated away
If one is found to abide by the rules,
They're labelled as square, certainly not 'cool'.

'Honesty is the best policy', in past time quoted.
Disgrace is old fashioned, if one is demoted.
The commandments once revered are a matter for scorn.
As foolishness to the headstrong, giving no thought to the morn.

Reaping the harvest from seed blown astray.
Suffering consequences of ill deeds done yesterday
Humanity does strive for a semblance of peace.
Seldom it's found, unless warring factors cease.

In the heart of mankind there's an aching space,
A craving for satisfaction to conquer this race,
Only one person can help us fulfil essential need
Jesus Christ, God's son, the author of peace.

Annie Harcus, Orkney, Scotland

PAINTING WITH WORDS

The hand moves, and the pen writes
From brain to hand, to paper bright,
He paints a picture with words that flow,
So others may read and come to know,
He writes of beauty, also of love
Of the earth beneath and the skies above.

The pen writes of the rich and poor,
About the deep valleys and dark moor's
Summer, Autumn, Winter and Spring,
Discussing what each season will bring.
He mentions the trees and flowers,
Of many gardens and happy hours.

To the writer, the whole world seems his,
With his words to us, he then happily gives,
A picture painted for you and me,
One that we can read and see.
What a wonderful world he has found,
And, with his words we are shown around.

Philomena Malik, Glasgow, Scotland

THESE WONDERFUL PEOPLE

Can you ever imagine how it must feel
To be born with eyes that cannot see
or to be born deaf or dumb
It is beyond our way of thinking
I am sure you will agree.

Not to see
Is trying to understand what a colour is and why
Not to hear,
is not to hear the sound of music, laughter or a baby cry.
Not to speak
But be able to communicate by sign language, writing or
lipreading
If you try.

There are many kinds of disabilities, yet
Those born with them, are always so happy
And never sad
They tell you, how can you miss what other people have
got, when that is the thing, you have never had.

Edward Biggins, Glasgow, Scotland

Edward Biggins said: "I started writing verse when very
young. I was always scribbling on paper notepads to pass
the time." My poems are influenced by the beauty and
goodness I see in people. I would describe my style as down
to earth. I am 63 years old, divorced with four children,
three girls and one boy, all grown up and I have three
grandchildren. I was born in Cambuslang. My hobbies
include playing the electric organ, singing, drawing car-
toons, writing songs and making artificial flowers. I would
like to meet fellow Scot Sean Connery and be John Travolta
for a day. My ambitions is just to see people happy."

MOTHER

I have often sat and wondered
What it would be like
To talk like we used to
And remember every night
And as I watch you fading
From the person you used to be
Into another world
And far away from me.

Your memories have all been taken
Now there's nothing left for you
Dementia is the cruelest thing

"Why did God give it to you?"

Helen McAlinden, Airdrie, Lanarkshire

UNTITLED

Standing on the train
I feel your arm around me.

Waiting at the crossroads
You breathe gently upon my neck.

In the middle of a conversation
I hear you laughing.

I shut my eyes
And know you're watching me.

My stomach churns and hollows
At the miles that separate us.

Ingrid Perch-Neilsen, Lentran, Inverness

THE MOONS-EYE VIEW

You call me cold, you know me not!
You only see me from afar,
I am no match for Sun so hot.
Nor will I ever be a star!

But where would you - Young Lover be
Without my light to guide you-
When you're strolling by the sea,
Or walking through the evening dew?

And you- Old poet, with your dreams,
Think of summer- think of June!
Re-live once more romantic scenes,
Without a doubt you'll think of 'moon'!

Or you, young Writer of Romance,
Your head is filled with lunar-lines:
"Come join me in a moon-light dance!"
Or: "See the moonlight through the pines!"

Oh, yes, I see much stolen love,
And thieves who work by night,
I see you all from high above;
I am your lunar-light.

Peter Jeevar, Castle Douglas, Scotland

NIGHT

Night is approaching
Darkness claws the light away,
With great talons of shadow,
It covers the land in a cloak of calm.

The moon is the only light,
It's great cavernous mouth,
Open in a silent scream,
Watching night swallow the earth below.

It touches every house, room and street,
Flooding them with darkness,
Smothering light,
Until dawn when the sun reigns again.

Jenny Hood, Aberdeen, Scotland

THE VOICE

Now a shiver of sadness spreads its wings
Across the Homeland, to America and beyond.
The Voice is stilled, and with its passing, brings
Back memories of triumphs, and standing room only.
The Voice, in all its richness held them fast,
Encompassing in its spell more, than mere stage presence,
Communicating with an audience-
Yes, by something indefinable, they were in trance.
Passing years saw the Voice much thinner grow,
And the strangest thing of all, the public wanted more.
Imitators were many, all around,
Lacking originality they went unnoticed.
Captured on C.D. the magic of the
Voice will live again, both here at home and overseas,
Reaching out to the sick and the lonely
Still surviving, for those who want to listen to it.

Alexander Winter, Aberdeen, Scotland

GLASGOW STREET SONG

Fan-daby-dozy
Ring-a-ring o' rosy
Young men pick thaur brides,
While auld men pick thaur noses,
We play knock-door-run up each aithers closes,
Hr auld man got the polis,
'Cos we called him skinny-ma-link,
The short sighted gink
Yew and mi behind the 'bike sheds'
Whaur we'll meet the ither neddies,
And beat the hell oot o' oor teddies,
Ma brither's big like Gavin Hastings,
And gives the ither kids sum pastings,
Hiv'e mit the big fat wummin who lives doon oor lane,
I'm Gaun in noo'
For I think its gonna rain.

Alan Pow, Hawick, Roxburghshire, Scotland

Alan Pow said: "I am aged 41 and live in Hawick in the Scottish Borders. I live with my parents, and am registered disabled. I write poetry as a hobby. I also like painting and drawing. I have had quite a few of my poems published and have written four plays which were performed in May 2001. Other poets influence my work. I have always had a vivid imagination. I try to write on subjects that interest me. I would most like to meet and be for a day Robbie Williams. My ambition is to have my own art exhibition."

FIESTA BRAVA

The ballet of blood and the suit of lights
sank to its close with the bull black on the sand
and the tinselled swordsman strutted the ring
under a hail of flowers, hats, oles
clutching a gristly ear and a red rose
embracing cheers for skill dancing with death
for grace with cloth and neatness with the steel.

Blind eyes turned from the crowd, nostrils in the sand
the bull ignored the music, pointing his horns
as handles for the horses, jingling with tin bells
that strained the ropes to drag him from the ring.
And a dragonfly, shimmering in the sunlight
swooped hawklike over the blood on the sand
and rose again over the heads and voices.
A glimmer of brightness sped off into the evening.

Nigel Grant, Glasgow, Scotland

KITT

My parents dog, he was the best,
He became their child, when their daughters flew the nest
Always faithful, loving and true.
A son he became and doted on them too.

From a small pup to his full size,
He could melt someone's heart with one look from his dole-
ful eyes
Ever youthful he was contented to stay by the fire and laze
And sometimes he could be seen sitting in an innocent
daze.

His hair was beautiful and shiny,
Ears like velvet, and teeth like a baby,
He chewed his food thoroughly, and occasionally was so
stubborn, he drove my parents crazy.

Although he has gone now, he'll never be forgotten
In his life, love was exchanged and no day
in his company was rotten.

Susan McGregor, Dundee, Scotland

THE PARK

As I walk my dog round the park.
I look around in wonder and awe
Not at the actual park, lovely though it is.
With its big green fields and over lapping trees and branch-
es.

I look at what is in the park
Young children playing on the swings and swimming in the
pool
Boys playing football and girls with their dolls
Young Mothers talking in crowds and Fathers standing at
the side.

As I walk a little further,
I see older people sitting on benches talking quietly
And elderly couples kissing discreetly on the cheek while
walking hand and hand.

As I walk forward I see an old tree.
With an knife crafted heart shape engraved on it,
Its marked with the initials AW loves EA 1932.

And I realise that the park symbolises ongoing life.
Because its a place where people feel comfortable
regardless of their age or sex.

Lesleyanne Crawford, Galashiels, Selkirkshire

REFLECTIONS

Looking in the large rectangular mirror
On the wall in the lounge
She sees, not her own image, but
The reflections of the garden
With the trees as a backdrop, beyond
It all looks more beautiful there
It has a fairytale quality about it.
The foliage is shimmering silver
And the cottonwool clouds are busy
Weaving their design in the sky.
The sun is there somewhere
Trying its best to peep through.
The pond glistens in its own corner
With the waterlilies
Languidly lazing on the surface
And the mass of fading pink and blue hydrangea
Is an artists's fantasy-
A place of mystery!

Joyce Anderson, Inverness, Inverness-shire

A DAYDREAM

In a magical world far away,
The sun will rise,
To start the day,
As a fairy files
To a hidden place,
Where a secret they keep
In that fabled place
Where magic does sleep.
Magic and colour splash,
Out to the wood,
Where elves and gnomes dash,
To fulfull the duties they believe they should.
Cherish this moment because it won't always stay,
Sigh as this lovely vision drifts slowly away.

Claire Loudon, Kirkintilloch, Scotland

SPIRALLING AVENUES

An intricate web of detail lies ahead,
I scale it now, lying here in my bed,
Frightening pastures seen through youthful gleam,
painting everything gold, or so it would seem,
a,h the bitter sweet taste of uncertainly rises,
plastered with secrets and hidden prizes,
where usually the pursuit itself is its own reward,
the chance to take your desired path forward,
yet, pray, nothing is quite as it seems
the road is cobbled that leads to your dreams
people fill your thoughts, can steal your heart away,
forbidden spices can easily lead you astray,
so don't be fooled by their talk of need,
the fools paradise lurks near - take head.

Claire McKenzie, Irvine, Ayrshire

THE WHEEL OF LIFE

Hamsters, running round their little wheel
As you watch their antics make you feel
They're going nowhere, running on the spot
Indeed the distance covered might not seem a lot

What about the human race in the year 2001?
We're also running, but we're having lots of fun!
Running to keep up this modern world's pace
Life appears so wonderful but is that the case?

An industry has evolved born just for you and me
To deal with all the stress we have, so you and I can be
Ready to make more bucks, go and buy designer gear
We have to keep out there in front because we really fear

What would happen if our life went into second gear
If it really slowed down, yet what have we to fear
I'm sure that most of us would love to halt that wheel
Get life back, relax once more, and do a slowed down reel!

Margaret Milne, Aberdeen, Grampian, Scotland

LARGE WOMAN

A busy restaurant made me share a table.
I enquired, 'A free seat?' and stopping her chat with the
waitress,
The large blonde woman said, 'Yes', and I settled into my
solitude.

But in the background I heard chat,
'Going to adopt her. She's no one else. Couldn't let her go
now.'
And I saw in the crook of the large woman's arm
A small baby, a tube emerging from her nose.

Time to go, the still baby zipped into warmth
Cosseted for outside February, the woman laughed
Into the baby's face and kissed her on the lips.
Passiveness gone, the small face filled with life,
A smile, the eyes bright for a large woman.

Doreen Presly, Newport-on-Tay, Fife, Scotland

SEE BUT UNSEEN

When I'm in my darkest depths your laugh provides a light,
When I'm feeling left out in the cold your warmth provides
a home,
When I feel like I have no choice your understanding shows
me different,
When I'm feeling low your persistence finds my smile,
When I'm having a bad day your energy provides me with
strength to carry on,
When I feel like I've reached the end your humour shows
me tomorrow,
When I feel so alone your shadow lets me know you'll be
there,
When I'm faced with uncertainty your belief gives me sup-
port,
When I feel like my dreams are unreachable your courage
enables me to try,
When I need your time your generosity you give away for
free,
When I have a problem your ingenuity always helps to
solve,
With my eyes and heart I see you so clearly,
Is it only with your eyes that you'll ever see me?

Elaine Donaldson, Peterhead, Aberdeenshire

THE SOUL OF A POET

A poet's words, come from the heart
from a myriad of feelings, emotions
suffered, good and bad. Wealth or
poverty, human conditions, makes people
what they are, poets telling in song
or rhyme, experiences borne with fortitude

Poets write in prose or rhyme, of this
world of men and women. love and hate,
warning of destruction, with hope of
rebirth, a poet, feels, more than most,
telling in song or rhyme, experiences
borne with a fortitude.

The poets souls, longing for love, without
heartache, seeking beauty, in song or rhyme
making this world a better place, for
for future generations. forget hate or
jealousy, and unkind thought, telling in
in song or rhyme, experiences, borne with
with fortitude.

Janet Middleton, Falkirk, Scotland

THE MAN IN THE WHITE COAT....

The man in the white coat
Is in my dream!
The man in the white coat,
Hears me scream.

The man in the white coat
"Doesn't care!"
He makes me stand
in my underwear.

The man in the white coat,
watches how I walk.
He prods and pokes,
While his colleagues talk.

He stretches my legs,
And bends my knee.
"Don't expect too much!"
He says of me.

"Men in white coats
Should sell ice cream!"
But my man in the white coat
Makes me scream!

Paul Anthony Heneachon, Prestwick, Ayrshire

WHAT HAS HAPPENED TO MY LITTLE GIRL

What has happened to my little girl
Wherever can she be?
What has happened to that girl
Who was all the world to me?

What has happened to that little doll
In tight jeans, socks and who played football?
I tell you brother it just isn't fair
Why, only yesterday I know she was there!

Now she's a pint sized venus overnight
Boy she's some sight-
Make up, high heel, curled up hair!
Yes she's alright.

But what has happened to my little girl-
Wherever can she be?
Tho' I still love this lovely teen-age queen,
I'd like my little girl back with me.

ElizaJane McNally, Alloa, Clackmannanshire

Dedicated to my youngest sister Margaret (Sleith) who inspired it.

WOUNDED SKIES

Wounded skies up high above
That looks down on our world with love,
White fluffy clouds that turn to grey
Crying tears that fall our way.

Our sins rise up to stab your heart
Tearing is apart each day,
But your love for us, mends the crying flesh
And sins are washed away.

When we hurt one another, we strike at you
Piercing the skies of a beautiful blue,
Your tear drops, falling to earth as rain
Forgive us lord, for causing you pain.

Your sunshine fills our hearts with glee
Beaming down on us,
Our sins are black, against your rays
But you always glisten through.

If only we could shine like you
And be as a calm blue sea,
Waves lapping gently against the sand
Forgiveness washing, around the land.

Mary Crowder, Perth, Scotland

MY SON

Will my son ever take a wife?
To make him happy all his life,
He's handsome and shy,
And good in every way,
And I wander why he's still with me today.

I love him dearly
As a mother can
But he is still with me yearly
And he's such a handsome man.

He's thirty years old.
and has a good wage.
He's quiet not bold,
and never gets in a rage.

At last my son has got a wife
A lovely girl is she,
I hope he'll be happy all his life,
What will be will be.

Betty Greig, Aberdeen, Scotland

REQUIESCAT

The grind of emotional traffic hurts my mind.
Eyelids dwindle shut, before tapering in
Molten trails, resting in the recesses of my face.
Road signs for the psyche.

I swirl my thoughts around in the
Mediterranean's bubbling blood, absorbing the
Age-old sage of the Sun through my hungry pores.
My seaweed-strewn doppel ganger soaks in all sound.

In this clamouring silence, I am unaware that my
Grief is for the loss of nothing -
You were never really there,
Just an impostor swathed in your skin.

I pour myself over the rock,
Am washed away by the rabid tide,
And, dispersing into azure molecules,
Network my way to Africa.

Michaella Docherty, Bellshill, Lanarkshire

THOUGHTS OF LOVE

Thoughts of love come flooding back,
of times so long ago
Thoughts of love just like the sea,
continue to ebb and flow.
Love is born throughout the seasons,
There is no rhyme, there are no reasons.

Thinking back I remember, warm sunny days,
Kisses so sweet, under soft moonlit rays.
Four seasons of joy, held deep in my heart.
Thoughts of love I recall, never to part.

I loved you then as I love you now,
I wish I could have shown you how.
You will always mean so much to me,
Please understand why I now set you free.

Hoping you will think of me,
And realise it had to be.
Deep down we knew that it would end,
To you fond wishes I do send.

Thoughts of love who I wanted to be,
Thoughts of love now so clear to me.
Thoughts of love of a happy life,
Thoughts of love but never a wife.

Liz Wilson, Aberdeen, Scotland

EBONY TO EMERALD EYES

The fear in your dark eyes
Shone like a panther
Reflecting black ebony
Stoney fearsome and cold

As you were ubruptly confronted
With a despiteful
Ghostly like figure
Disappearing into the night

With shining eyes of green
Shimmering stones of emeralds
Haunting the soul
Jewels of demonism

Piercing sharp arrows
As the apparition narrows.

Ann Copland, Aberdeenshire, Scotland

ORDINARY GUY

Here I sit a little perplexed
A lesser mortal might be vexed
Why do it this thing that I do
What are the consequences that may ensue
Sitting here trying to gather my thoughts
Thinking up some worthwhile plots
What drives me to commit these linguistic acrobatics
When life's already filled with such amateur dramatics
Is it a challenge, to try to be good
Or is it just that my thoughts need some food
It's not even that I've got such a lot to say
Not too many ideas in this head to betray
It's not that I'm an extrovert nor even a little shy
I'm me, just an ordinary guy.

Alan Milby, Wigtownshire, Scotland

TIME FOR LOVE

This watch is for our love together, Nan,
although I know that every tick appears
to clip a vital second from your span,
that seconds grow to minutes, then to years.
And as the years roll by, will you forget
that once we two were lovers for a while,
or will it be as though we'd never met,
and never shared a sorrow, shared a smile?
Will I be able to recall each day
at will an image of your bonny face,
or will the faithless mind at last betray,
and passing years the memory erase?

The future minds itself, and has to be,
blind time ticks on and on, remorselessly.

Ken Angus, Midlothian, Scotland

A CITY SCENE

The morning sun strikes yellow in my room
Through windows laden with the dusty city air.
I rub the sleep from dark unrested eyes,
And stare unseeing at the papered desk.

Outside, the grey and roofless corridors
Stretch to distant indistinction,
Filled with smoke and sound and fury
And a wall-to wall carpeting of cars.

The early mail brings urgent messages
Written in haste by other weary men,
Varying in their vocabulary, but not
In their monumental insignificance.

How can it be that man has brought himself,
Willing to this monotony of days,
Where nothing separates the miracle from the mundane
Except, of course, a decision to publish.

Bill Sylvester, Inverness, Scotland

THE WINTER OF MY LIFE

And as dusk falls, this ancient knights still roams,
His territory much smaller than before,
With armour wearing thin, and sword less honed
He's finally forced to bow to nature's law.
Weaker now, he prefers to ride alone,
Only his words can still cut to the bone.
His trusty steed looks tired, in need of rest
Perhaps this time, the animal knows best.
As gnarled hands lose their grip of days gone by
He looks less at the land, and more the sky,
The era of this knight is at an end,
He could move on, but finds he cannot bend.

Graham Anderton, Orkney, Scotland

Graham Anderton said: "I live on the Orkney Islands, where I run a small farm. I am happily married with four children and, my search for adventure and freedom has led me into the wildest areas of Britain and Canada. Still very active and a competitive sportsman, I retain a deep love for the countryside and its wildlife. I began writing poetry several years ago, and have recently published my first book "Life Runs Through It," a selection of poems and true stories. It can be ordered online www.Orkneybook.co.uk price £15.95 plus p&p."

A PAIR

Weary arms they lay down
As angels folding wings
In the passages of darkness
They are a pair

Under a starry lintel
They breathe as one
Their white breaths
Rise to catch the frost

Barely they hear
The agony of the trees
The raping wind
In the night grass.

The moon crafts they
Silhouettes of pure silver
In churchyard grace
They are a pair.

Mike Monaghan, Bishopbriggs, Scotland

TO A FRIEND WITH MOTORNURON DISEASE

As he lay there in his hospice bed
Who knew what thoughts were in his head
Did he think of his family and his wife
Or, of the things he'd failed to do in life.

As I looked at him lying there.
His face expressionless, his body an empty shell.
I wondered what his thoughts were,
As the tears in my eyes began to well.

As I sat there and spoke with him,
Of the things we had seen and done.
But now his body was so weak and thin
And death would slowly come.

His time on earth was drawing nigh
And we knew, that soon he would die
He looked so peaceful, no pain that we could tell,
And death released him, from his hell.

George Wright, Auchinleck, Scotland

A CAT'S EYE VIEW

Why do humans take off their fur
and immerse themselves in water
when all you need is tooth and claw
to keep your coat in order

They seem to use such strange objects
a litter tray that make noises
things to push, things to pull
things that are noisy or glow with light
life is much more simple for a cat

All I need is a place to sleep
a place to scratch
or for other needs
entertainment I can find all around me,

Katrina Heintz, Bathgate, Scotland

EARLY MORNING

I love the early morning
When there's nobody around
Wakened by the dawn chorus
Dew upon the ground.

The rising sun comes over the hill
Its peaceful quiet, calm and still
Hearing the birds sweetly sing
Contemplating what the day might bring

Early morning for me alone
No callers at the door, no telephone
In the silence I love to pray
Then I'm ready to face the day.

Wilma Barrett, Peebles, Scotland

AUTUMN TURNS TO WINTER

Orange turns to silver and then to bare
It's wet and it's sunny at the same time
It's beautiful and yet it's that time of year
When everything dies and turns to mush
It's dark most of the time yet so many colours
Surround us during the day so when night
Comes around it's colour is black and
We forget the gold rainbows left behind
For in a short time it will all disappear
Leaving only the skeleton of nature once more
But don't sleep during the winter months
They have a joy of their own
And very soon spring will be born.

Pat Braden, Carrickfergus, Antrim

THE VOICE IN THE WILDERNESS

I heard a voice call my name.
A voice in the wilderness.
And I turned to see who it was,
It was you and you said
"Come to me"
And I came as you called my name
For I knew you, and you knew me
And we were one, with the one
Who is, who said, "I am"
And the voice in the wilderness
Calls to you, as he called to me?
Turn to see, if the call to you
Is the same, as it was to me?
Turn to see, if you know him,
As he knows you, as he knows me
For he was called,
The voice in the wilderness.

Aidan Mills, Strabane, Tyrone

ALL AT SEA

This house of stone
Stands here alone
Grey solid square.
It looks out there
Across the bay
Where twice a day
It would appear
The sea's too near.

The night comes soon.
There is no moon.
You watch the beach
Just out of reach
And hear the roar
Upon the shore.
Will all be well?
You cannot tell.

But if you're wise
You'll close your eyes
And go to sleep
A sleep so deep.
An unseen hand
Has it all planned.
The tide will go.
Don't worry so.

Brenda Brown, Castletown, Isle Of Man

ATOMIC LULLABIES

The war that rages in some far-flung sky
Not yours to fight, not yours to wonder why
You couldn't change this bitter, twisted world
The welcome mat for you is not unfurled
You know the holocaust is your domain
You know that life will never stay the same
A good night kiss dropped on your furrowed brow
Will sooth away the hurt of here and now
Lullabies on ether softly lilting
While Armageddon's edifice to earth is tilting
Entrust your hopes and fears to caverns deep
And face the fire that fuels such restless sleep
This maelstrom rage far across the land
Atom bombs will fall from heaven's hand
With utter disregard for our distaste
Will lay these comfort blankets all to waste
So keep tight hold of just one precious thing
And bless your dreams with lullabies I sing
When the winds of change have blown your ship aground
Let these atomic lullabies lay you down.

Vanessa Rivington, Dollingstown, County Down

REARRANGE

I have hidden my emotion,
Suffered with devotion.
And I hope that I am changing,
I hope you'll rearrange me.
And I've always been left standing,
Or flying round but never landing.
And my back hurts from the lifting,
Of stumbling blocks for my tripping.

When I find I'm in a big top,
Dressed in stripes with an alarm clock.
I hope that I'll be woken,
By your words so softly spoken.
When I swear I'm in a castle,
In my element with no hassle.
Don't be scared to say I'm lying,
Either way I'll still keep trying.

Now it seems that you are waiting,
You really want me, no more chasing.
And I hope that I am changing,
I hope you'll rearrange me.

Simon Maltman, Bangor, County Down

Simon Maltman said: "I have been writing poetry for a
good few years and have been published with United Press
before, as well as making my own little booklet. I also write
for my band - Bound [www.Bound-uk.4t.com] and we are
involved in the local scene. This poem is really just about
falling in love with someone and letting them inside. This
poem is special to me because of what it reminds me of."

THE LONELY BUSH

The wind whispered in the park.
Whispered hush! hush! hush!
Playing with the branches,
On the thorny, lonely bush.

How many years it's standing there,
I've heard no-body say.
Do not disturb the lonely bush
Or take its life away!

Marian T McGrath, Belcoo, Northern Ireland

GIFTS

Say you've no gifts from the father
Feel you are worthless, no good
These thoughts don't come from the saviour
He loves you as no one could.

Sit quietly, listen to Jesus
Then he will speak so sweet
Of the gift that came from Mary
When in love, she washed his feet

He'll tell of the sisters welcome
Into their home where he ate
Opened their door to many
That day with Jesus, they met

You do have gifts from the father
In love he gives by his grace
So many gifts he will mention
On that day, you see his face.

Patricia Kelly, Bangor, County Down

BE MY GUIDE

William you may wonder lonely on a cloud;
It's doubtful, for your nature loving
Heart would thrive up there.
I cheekily request you be my guide,
As I strive to pit my puny pen and
Creep in your mighty footsteps.
I gaze into a pinpricked shadow
Before the sun, which rises like
A curtain in the morn,
Searching for a wisp of the
Gleam you possessed for
Inspiration and turn of phrase,
That would make you proud,
Reflect you at your best.

Roseanna Tyrrell, Tullamore, Offaly

WHISPERS IN THE MOONLIGHT

At night the shadows walk
The streets.
In the corners you don't
See.
At night the trees whisper
Your name.
As you walk through the
Park.
At night the moon watches
The lady out walking.
Not realising she's being
Watched.
At night the owls fly between
The stars.
Searching.

Jodie McQueen, Richhill, Armagh

LONELY HOST

The grave-yard
An unwanted lonely host
Mother of a dead-number
Speaking only of unwanted-slumber
And, the stilled dance of yesterday's beloved ghost
A place for natures dead
A place for innocent-victims to softly tread
A place for civilised life to eternally pause
A place for the scattered debris...
Of mad man's revolutionary cause
A place to pass-by, if not required there
For the dead-are-dead,and must be exiled
And the living and the under-world...
Cannot be reconciled
A place where all sinking coffins...
And all of the unblinking dead-lives,
Are invisibly the same
Imprisoned colour-codes of the past
Dead, and already isolated...
From any present or future democratic life-game.

William McKeen, Belfast, Antrim

Aged 63 **William McKeen** enjoys writing, supporting Manchester United, and community activities. He was born in Belfast and started writing in 1976. "I did it to provide an alternative to the daily depression of Ulster politics, and the murder of a family member," he explained. "Almost anybody trying to be creative has influenced my work and I would describe my style as street commentary. I would like to be remembered as an honest street thinker. My mission is to see a higher philosophy in mankind." He is married to Hannah and they have four children, Deborah, Angela, William and Neil. "The person I would most like to be for a day is Robinson Crusoe and the people I would most like to meet are all of mankind's victims to apologise to them." William has written many poems and had several published.

NO DEGREE NEEDED

And that's to you young pessimist:
The world's a dreadful place, I know.
The virus spreads. The cure is slow.
Another body is dismissed
from chains and hypocritical glow
which keeps the aids and money flow.
The moving star has lost its place
and touches big and small and tall
and leaves us with some false sensation.
Your sentence is death! What about probation?-
Give it chance in this courtly case!
It will change slowly, with, in, and through you-after all.

Iris Ferrier, Douglas, Isle Of Man

THE FORGOTTEN SOLDIER

As I lie here in this strange and foreign place
Soft morning rain falls upon my face.
Faint noise I hear of distant guns,
The battles o'er but never won.

All around young men lie in death's sweet sleep
As I, all alone I weep,
Darkness comes no comfort be.
No one will come to rescue me.

My wound is deep but feel no pain
I will not see my love again
My eyes grow dim, no more dreams to chase,
As I die here in this strange and foreign place.

Helen M'Shane, Limavady, Londonderry

THE FALL

I broke my fingers on yer bottle,
Spitting words through the curtain with my headache.
I arched my back and was not extensive,
But transferred to the corner repenting.
The splitting of paradise set my teeth on edge
And gave me away.

I broke my deal on yer arrival,
Screaming for fig leaves to give me protection,
Gaining no comfort recalling the union:
'Let the noise hide me or I'll peel like an onion!'
And I saw the landscape only as a mist,
The garden only as a sword.

I broke my teeth on yer rejection,
Seeing the coffin dropped down into the future.
I fought for darkness but night came along instead,
And only in the morning light did I see that you were dead.
The birth pangs begin as Adam lays down his head
And it all starts over again.

Mark Niblock, Bangor, County Down

HAPPINESS

Happiness is peace of mind and contentment,
Happiness is giving up to resentment.
Happiness in contemplation
Give up thinking, try meditation.
You'll reach Nirvana, then there'll be a
Celebration.
You'll be in a permanent state of elation.
Don't let your ego digress
That will depress.
Just lengthen the gap between the thoughts,
Your Nirvana will then be brought.

Peter Goodall, Antrim, Northern Ireland

Born in Belfast **Peter Goodall** enjoys meditation, computing, reading and music. "I started writing poetry when I saw a programme on Robert Graves, the famous poet," explained Peter. "It showed how he was inspired by meditation and I decided to give it a try. My work is influenced by meditation, God and romantic inspiration and I would describe my style as romantic and inspirational. I would like to be remembered as a good friend to everyone who knows me and someone who cared for and helped others. That's what we are all here for." Aged 54 he is a carer with an ambition to reach Nirvana or marry the love of his life. "The person I would most like to meet is the Dalai Lama, as he inspires so much happiness," added Peter who says that his biggest fantasy is to levitate.

ABSENCE

Explaining what love has and does
Is hard to do.
For love is not solid matter,
It is only a mere feeling for someone or something.
So with no physical weight or shape
It cannot be described
As it gives you nothing.
Yet it has great effects on people and their lives.
One thing that lovers and those who don't love know is,
Love will only break hearts
But the absence of love will break lives.

Suzi Batchelor, Omagh, Tyrone

Born in Belfast **Suzi Batchelor** enjoys music, sports, sailing, dancing, conversation and singing. "I started writing poetry because I felt it was the only way I could to get my feelings across to people," she said. "My work is influenced by people around me and my classmates and my style involves abstract romanticism. I would like to be remembered for my sense of humour and as a loyal friend." Aged 14 she is a schoolgirl with an ambition to study medicine. "The person I would most like to be for a day is the singer Christina Auguilera and I would love to meet Brian Clough because I am a lifelong Nottingham Forest supporter," she added.

MOTHER AND CHILD

To be allowed to enter
Watch and feel the love.
Between a Mother embracing
And child-beloved one.
Natural depth off emotion
Unquestioned togetherness-clung.
As in visual unison
A praise eternally unsung.

With caresses cherished
Bestowed in undying devotion.
As blessed from above
Embroidered from above
Embroidered in magic potion.
Between a Mother embracing
And child-her beloved one.
As in visual unison
A praise eternally-unsung.

Gary Finlay, Tralee, Kerry

THE PRICELESS ELGIN MARBLES OF THE BRITISH MUSEUM

Lord Elgin was Brit Ambassador
To the place...Constantinople.
Venetian siege did damage:
But the marbles stayed classic and noble.
Origins...round 444 bc.
Brits made proper purchase with permission....
But the Turks were controlling Athens then
So was there pressurised submission?
Today's parliamentary legislation
Prevents disposal of such art....
Ostensibly allowing scholarship
Every day of week long after dark.
The Parthenon sculptures are the best loved treasures
Of the museum's exibitions...
Forms framed in genius for all the world
Despite some Greek opinions.
No limits across time or place
Can be placed upon the Elgin marbles,
But great 'good will' would surely generate
If they could be an 'EXHIBIT' where they started.

Robert John Moore, Belfast, County Down

To Elefteria Tsakalov. This is my attempt to fulfil the tongue in cheek promise to deliver her the Elgin marbles.

AN EXILE LONGING FOR HOME

As a child I watched the swallows come and go from year to
year.
And I thought some day I'll join them-I'm tired of living
here
I made my plans and started out, just happy to be free
I thought the world's my oyster, this is the life for me
When I saw Ayres Rock by moonlight and MT Fuji in
Japan.
My thoughts went home to Donard and the snows on the
Slievenamann
When I stood at the Grand Canyon in the blistering desert
heat
I thought of dear Glenelly's gentle slopes and wandering
sheep
Niagra Falls are awesome with their thundering deafening
roar
But I'd rather hear the ripple of the brook in Tollymore
Why am I here in exile with this heat and dust and flies?
Its spring at home in Armagh, soft rain falling from the
skies
I will travel down to Sydney and book on the next flight
My minds made up, I must go home indeed I'll go tonight.

Norah Burnett, Richhill, Armagh

PALMY DAYS

Let us not grieve in wintry gloom,
Now that the autumn leaves are gone,
Few ever saw the summer bloom,
As you and I have done.

Let us not pine for radiant days,
Now that the clouds are an ashen hue,
Few ever basked in those tropic rays
That you and I once knew.

Let us not weep nor be full of sadness,
Now that the birds no longer call,
Few even heard those songs of gladness,
You and I recall.

Let us rejoice for warm days gone by,
Now it is dark December,
Few ever glimpsed the azure sky,
That you and I remember.

Let us give thanks that we heard the band,
Now the parade is a distant dream,
Few ever marched through that magic land,
Where you and I have been.

Nicolas Byrne, Welshpool, Wales

TO THE MEMORY OF ROBERT GRAVES

Here was a man
left for dead,
but survived....

In disgrace-
went to live
on foreign isle.

What a poet!
Moves one to tears,
(love inspires).

What learning,
(erudition).

Goodbye to all that.........

Geraint Jenkins, Barry, Wales

Geraint Jenkins said: "I am a much married (three times) octogenarian, who lives alone at present in a very nice flat in my home town of Barry, in South Glamorgan. I have wide interests and writing is only one of them: I got into it by accident almost, lacking confidence at first, but gaining it rapidly now thanks to United Press! As a humanist, I have been influenced by many authors, events and circumstances, and describe my style as 'realistic and objective,' though this doesn't mean that it isn't affected by those 'inner forces' which are so difficult to define, but which drive people to express depths of thought and feeling."

SPECTRUM

Roses are red, violets are blue,
Labour or Tory which one are you?
Liberal lemon, bright and benign
A party that seems to have so much time.
Then there are some who want to come clean
Challenge our thinking turn the world green.
All things considered, a rainbow'd be best
Cover the spectrum, unite in the quest
To find some solutions and give us some rest.

Lynda Howell, Haverfordwest, Wales

Lynda Howell said: "I am an elocutionist whose love and
empathy for the spoken word reflects in my successful elo-
cution practice. I live at the heart of the beautiful county
of Pembrokeshire, and am very aware of the timelessness,
constancy, and grandeur of the seascapes, mountains and
ancient monuments which form so much a part of my daily
life. Married with three children, who now follow their own
individual professions, I have, since the tragic death of my
second daughter, found expression for my grief and faith in
the future through my poetry."

FOR MY WIFE

I hate you I miss you I love you
You're the worst, you're okay, you're the best
A moment, a marriage, a lifetime
To agree, to abstain, to contest
My brainwaves, my heartbeats, my soul wings
The womb, the wound, the grave
I hate you, I miss you, I love you
This master, this pupil, this slave.

Martin Faulkner, Lower Cwm, Wales

UNDERSTAND

If one limps you must not stare as he goes down the road,
Perhaps the pack upon his back is to much of a load.
Just thank the Lord for what you got and you don't want to
lose,
And also say a thank you that you don't wear his shoes.

Perhaps Gods burden on his back is a load he cannot
share,
And as he limps and carries on some people do not care.
The road he has to follow with the burden on his
back,
Maybe one day will lighten and his shoes may lose the
tacks.

Or maybe disability and you will never know, why that man
Limps and struggles on, and you just let him go.
So next time think and give a smile to that poor sole out
there,
Let him go on down his road but let him know you care.

James Hinder, Barry, Wales

TO UNCLE JOHN

You picked me a rose
In the summery air
You picked me a memory
To wear in my hair

You picked me a rose
From a magic tree
You climbed down the ladder
And gave it to me.

Rebecca Punter, Bridgend, Wales

Dedicated to Uncle John, the only one to pick me a yellow rose.

PATHS

There are many pathways as we walk lifes road
And we choose one carefully to attain our goal.
We are given patterns from an early birth
Set out by our parents who had found their worth.
There will be temptations, and though some may fall,
Bravely face the future, and obey the call.
Families are broken and the bitter pain
Shakes our very being as we feel the strain.
We must build foundations as we wend our way,
And be guarded always in the things we say.
There are many potholes which we must avoid
And control is vital when we are annoyed.
Life is never easy, but the message plain
Put in super effort, and you'll reap the gain.
There are many pathways, always choose the best
For a clear conscience make a perfect rest.

Glenys Moses, Sennybridge, Wales

THE NEWLY HATCHED

What a great space. How exciting. Cheep! You're alive, like
me, how wonderful. Cheep! cheep! cheep! I'm longing to
meet you and communicate, but you're ignoring me. Don't
I matter? I'm real, like you.

If only you would say, "Hello, welcome to the world." I'm in
your hand. It is warm and alive but you don't look at me.
That hard thing you push me onto is cold and unfriendly.
I'm real, like you. Don't you see me?

Alwyn Jolley, Llandudno, Wales

OPEN DOOR

You call me through your tears,
But I cannot mend your heart
What's done is done,
But do not let us part.

Keep the door open,
Because I am always near.
The day you least expect it,
I will quietly appear.

For now you must be patient,
And when you dry your tears.
I will come close and help you,
Chase away those fears.

Your longing is tenfold within
That cannot be denied.
So bring back those happy thoughts,
And no more shall you cry.

Irene Morgans, Treorchy, Wales

WHO ARE YOU?

What do you see
When you look in a mirror?
You see yourself
But I see a stranger

She stares at me
Like a zombie undead
Eyes stiff as a rock
Heavy as lead

Inside her I know
She's caring and kind
It will always show
Through her empty mind

She's not stupid
Her work isn't bad
Only sometimes she remembers
Why she is sad

She has a home
Food more than plenty
That's when she remembers
Stomachs are empty.

Dian Phillips, Porth, Wales

THE WELL WORN TRACK

I wandered along a well worn track,
Which crossed a stream by a shack,
Where sheep were gazing side by side
They looked up staring stoney eyed.

I rambled on knee deep in mud,
Passed fields of cows chewing the cud
Crossed bridges and climbed hillocks too
Pausing once to admire the view.

I walked on through woods to a bog
Which was surrounded by a green fog,
The air was clammy and very damp
I moved on quickly, lest I get cramp.

The wind picked up a little bit,
So there was just time to stop and sit
And watch the horses on higher ground,
Near old farm cottages scattered around.

The path zig zagged up hill, down dale
But now the sun had grown quite pale,
Its time to turn round and go back
Down along the well worn track.

Christine Williams, Culverhouse Cross, Wales

SWALLOW YOUR PRIDE

Mend those bridges before its too late
Send out your love instead of hate
Once one passes over to the other side
Regrets there will be, to late to cry.

So give that person a call today
You make the first move come what may,
It could be the beginning of a new life
Ending your fears, and years of strife.

Swallow your pride it will stifle you,
Maybe the other person is feeling blue too
Get together, start today
Give your hand in friendship, you show the way.

Lorna Culshaw, Portskewett, Wales

WAR

Why do people choose to fight
If only they could see the light
War is raging all around
A thunderous march is heard
Underground

People stand their with their guns
Shooting people just for fun
Countries at war all year round
Guns and screams are the only sounds

Why are people prepared to die
For a war which is full of lies
Children die at a sad young age
All because of a mad mans rage

Laura Neal, Mountain Ash, Wales

RAINBOWS

Pure light on sparkling water
Sending beams across the sky
Arching over hill and valley
Giving beauty to the eye.

Still we stand and gaze in wonder
As people did, so long ago,
Looking up at the creator
Painting skies with a coloured bow.

Though modern scientists explain it
That still does not take away
The miracle of Heavenly beauty
Painted on a sky of grey.

Pamela Evans, Maesteg, Wales

ROAD RAGE LET THE MONSTER GO

What's wrong with people,
driving cars like cages.
They are the wild animals inside,
a little bump or confusion
Sending them into rage,
a murderous look of hate.
A scorning scolding shake,
from caring mother
or loving brother,
to an evil monster of hate.
Just because of a metal cage,
Making their nasty secure.
Behaviour like that is primitive,
Concluding our fate,
As we remain, in a primeval state.

Lee Jones, Neath, Wales

CANCER

There is a disease and its not at all nice
but there are some people that have to pay the price
They need needles and jabs to help them along
at the end of the day it is very very long
Any food that you eat will make you feel sick
so you have to suck water from a lollipop stick
People do stare when you have no hair
When you're chemo's just finished another one starts
When you get to this part just sit back and say
I will get better today yes today
Good luck to you all whether you're big or small.

Brydie McDonald, Newport, Wales

MY DOG SABLE

She greets me every morning,
Stretching smiling and yawning.
Whenever I need a friend
On her I can always depend
Looking around she's always there,
When sometimes no one cares.
She loves to go for a walk,
She always listens when I need to talk.
She seems to know when I'm not well
It's strange how my dog can tell.
When I have to go away
By the back door she will stay.
There's a bond between us that will never die
I know one day I will have to say goodbye.
Until then she will be my best mate
For when the day comes I will hate.
But I will thank god for the times we had
And perhaps I won't feel so bad.

Sylvia Mudford, Newport, Wales

AFON ARGOED (WELSH VALLEY)

Woodland green, a sunny day, river rushing down below,
Foaming wavelets on their way, tumbling, leaping as they go.
Sound of water acts like balm, "sursuration" soothes the soul,
Bathes it all in heavenly calm, makes one feel renewed and whole.

Walking in the wooded dell, hearing bird calls all around
Seeing butterflies as well - Nature's blessings all abound.
Mounting up the fir-clad hill, valley vistas now unfold,
Climbing ever higher still, panoramic views untold!

Looking at the distant town from the heather- covered mount,
Human troubles far away seem to be of no account.
If you're stressed and need a break, then to hills and valleys go.
Soothing, ev'ry step you take - try it and you'll find it so.

Alan Wilson, Bryncoch, Wales

LOYAL FRIEND

One bitter December morning I found you gone
you must have drifted away in your sleep,
but in my heart the pain was so strong
the loss of your soul had cut me deep.

I stroked your body and anguished at the touch,
inside I was screaming please don't go from me,
I didn't realise that losing you would hurt so much,
I thought you would be here forever this I didn't foresee.

I often think of the long walks we would do together
you liked to run off but always kept me in your sight,
I assumed like these fields you would be around forever,
but now I watch for your shining star each night.

When ever your vision enters my thoughts I see,
the beauty of your soul that was lent to us for a while,
you were a loyal friend that stayed true to me,
and for that when I think of you it will be with a smile.

In loving memory of Taff

Emma Owen, Flint, Wales

GOD'S TEARS

I look out the window pouring rain
Rain every day it's a strain
The weather is changing with the years
God must be crying many tears

He can see his world below
Fighting and killing friend and foe
It's going back to the days of old
When men's hearts were icy cold

He's sending the rain rivers rise
He's trying to make us open our eyes
It can't go on destruction for gain
All it will do is bring us pain.

The rivers and fields joined as one
Mass areas of water towns over run
It's so depressing rain, rain, rain
Splashing against my window pane

God's crying floods as he looks down
Before too long we will all drown?
God's stopped crying the floods have gone
He must be pleased he's sent the sun.

Glenys Broxton, Welshpool, Wales

ONLY INSIDE

I hold myself together
With wishes and threads of desire
And unfounded promises in the future
That will maybe never come true

Still above all the broken dreams
And the cruel knowledge of how
Lonely and cold my inner soul is
Still I hope

Since my first breath I have waited for you
Always I have I searched
Into every face I have looked, with every touch
I wait for the thrill that never comes

Did I arrive too soon or too late?
You must be there somewhere
Or is the final irony that you too
Only exist in my imagination.

Ann Briggs, Swansea, Wales

IT'S ALL A MATTER OF SPECIFICS

It's love, love, it's all in the mind,
Where can I find love in my mind?
It's all a matter of specifics
If you find him it's terrific
He's walking down the road in
shocking pink.
It wouldn't be right if he was wearing mink?
His round head is like a ball and chain,
And his long hair has got a mane.

What is he doing? Is he catching a train?
If he is, he's not very vain?
Hark' I hear the train in the distance
Chug, chug, that's what it sounds like in the distance
It's love, love It's all in the mind,
The sound of a train is love' in my mind,
I'll walk down the tracks to meet my train
Finding love is not in vain'
Chug, chug, is the sound of the train.

It's all a matter of specifics
If you find him It's terrific.

David Rosser, Ammanford, Wales

83

AUNTIE DORIS

April eighteenth nineteen ninety nine
Is Doris birthday
The ram is her sign

Born in Ralph Cottage
With a harbour view
Having brother and sisters
Luxuries were few.

As years advanced
And war was declared
Brothers served the ranks
The sisters worked their share.

Later on with peace restored
And partner safely home from abroad
She moved to London
With her husband Doug
But the strings of the heart
To Tenby did tug.

A few years later they came back home
To Wales and family
Never more to roam.

Cheryl Phillips, Tenby, Wales

THE WISE MAN

I am too old to undertake this journey
Too old too tired, too sick at heart to care.
Why should I travel miles across the desert?
Why should I travel never knowing where?

There has been nothing in the uncaring heavens
Though I have scanned them long for untold years.
Many a dark night have I watched and listened
Straining to hear the music of the spheres

I have grown grey with weary hours of waiting
To see a new star blaze across the land
Searching with dimming eyes the ancient wisdom
Which has foretold Messiah is at hand.

The beckoning finger of the star commands me
Through I am old and sick at heart and mind,
It promises that I shall see and worship
At journey's end the King of all mankind.

Jean Adams, Abergavenny, Wales

FATHER

Churchyard yew trees, 'hundred strong,
Avenues - narrow, long,
Resting place for many years,
Sharing mem'ries, shedding tears.

Home town to my father dear,
Childhood haunts of yesteryear,
Gravel pathways, ancient halls,
Memorial, times recalled.

Father taken all too soon,
Relationship, a crescent moon,
Denied the fruits of later years
Silently we shed our tears.
In the shadows of our mind
Treasured memories we find,
And whilst I knew you as a boy
As man to man fate stole my joy.

Sharing prime time here with you,
Comforted in solitude.
In my mind you're always there
Tho' worlds apart, our lives we share.

Adrian Thomas, Chepstow, Wales

Adrian Thomas said: "I live in Chepstow with my wife Katrina
and last year published my first poetry collection entitled
"Reflections." Since the dawn of the new millennium I have been
writing regularly. Inspired by the world around me, I enjoy writ-
ing about nature and the beauty of creation and occasionally also
delve into more humorous verse usually inspired by my own mis-
fortune! Poetry provides freedom of expression and I like to use it
as a means of relaxation; thought-provoking and fulfiling.
"Reflections" is available @ £4.50 ISBN 1 86248 154 7."

CLOCKWORK DANCING

We met by chance, the maid and I
Autumn gold hair and oak green eyes.
Deep in the forest where no folk go
She whispered to me, her voice pitched low
'DON'T LIVE YOUR LIFE IN CLOCKWORK TIME.

When I grew up, no longer a boy
I ran with the Devil, wound up like a toy.
I forgot how to laugh, I forgot how to cry
The Devil shouted 'keep up or die.'
I LIVED MY LIFE IN CLOCKWORK TIME.

The clock ran down , I could run no more
Weary and broken I sank to the floor.
Helplessly watched as the dance passed me by
I remembered the maid and returned home to die
NO NEED NOW FOR CLOCKWORK TIME.

We met again, the maid and I
Autumn gold hair and oak green eyes
I stayed in the wood where no folk go
Finally at peace where Time doesn't flow.
CLOCKWORK TIME DIED.

Mal Phillips, Penygraig, Wales

OLD SHOE TO NEW

The old shoe is worn scuffed down at heel
The new shoe is shiny and full of appeal
The old shoe has trod the same path for years
The new shoe promises happiness not tears

The old shoe leaves what its known
The new shoe steps out on its own
The old shoe is tired the leather is faded
The new shoe has vigour not tainted or jaded

The old shoe looks sad its had its day
The new shoe looks happy to tread a new way
The old shoe has a history of sorrow
The new shoe has a future - a tomorrow

The old shoe leaves its past behind
The new shoe is going a new path to find
The old shoes my old job its been my past
The new shoe my new job happy at last

The old shoe has a worn sole
The new shoe has a new soul.

Nina Froley, Porthcawl, Wales

Born in Bridgend **Nina Froley** enjoys crosswords, walking and
reading. "I started writing poetry about ten years ago to express
my mood in verse," she explained. "My work is influenced by
everyday events and the world around me and my style is based
on simple observations of life. I would like to be remembered as a
person who works hard and delights in achievements, however
small." Aged 49 she is a shop assistant with an ambition to be
healthy, happy, and not to need to work as hard as she already
has. She is married to Brian and they have one son, Dean. "I
would like to have met Princess Diana because she was so won-
derful and I would like to meet Edward Heath because of his
interesting views. The person I would most like to be for a day is
Judith Chalmers because I love travel so much," she pointed out.
Nina has written many poems and had several published.

THE CRIPPLE WHO MARRIED THE BEAUTIFUL GIRL

As lovers they had skimmed stones on the romantic Roath
Park lake and walked down leafy wooden county lanes. She
was a pretty blonde with rectangular glasses and they went
for walks with his English sheepdog. On holiday in
Barbados they walked along deserted white sandy beaches,
him practicing walking with an artificial leg acquired in a
fight. She had enjoyed the devilish rape by the barbarian
who crippled him and stole her off him. But that was gone.
Just like 'Born Free' they were a couple returning to the
Serenghetti mating after disrobing in the sand. Kissing side
by side in the sand. It was 2122 AD and they flew up into
outer space in the Hotel Spacecraft. In the Caribbean
drinking pineapple juice from crystal tumblers. She recip-
rocated his fondness for her in spades. He was always with
her. He felt such an immediate urge to give her very des-
perate kisses on the lips.

Julian Gaius Williams, Ammanford, Wales

Born in Carmarthen **Julian Williams** enjoys writing, music
and TV. "I won first prize for a poem on a school cruise to
Spain at the age of 13," said Julian. "I would describe my
style as fluent and with flair. The person I would most like
to meet is Robert Vaughan, the actor. I would also like to
meet the Spice Girls because I'm fond of them. The person
I would most like to be for the day is my idol, Melvyn
Bragg." Julian has written many poems and had several
published. He has also written two books. Some of his
poems are available in bookshops worldwide (in Anthologies
of poetry).

SNOW ANGELS

Appearing overnight
A most glorious sight
Flakes descending swirling twirling

Gently touching one's face
Seemingly myriads of angels to embrace
Conveying a message to everyone
Goodwill on earth 2001

All having landed around
Forming snow white carpet on ground
Rosy cheeked children (ride toboggan)
in colourful caps with pompoms on
across each valley
folk daren't dilly dally
awesome sight from Heaven above
Blotts pollution while our creator beams his love.

Joan Rees, Mountain Ash, Wales

Born in South Wales **Joan Rees** started writing poetry only
a few years ago. "People prompted me to have a go and at
last I felt encouraged to put my thoughts on paper," she
explained. "My work is influenced by people, animals and
daily events and my style is pleasant. I would like to be
remembered for having devoted my life to caring for those
less fortunate and for being kind to animals which have
been treated cruelly." Aged 79 she is a retired nurse with
an ambition to write more poetry. She has had poems
published in the local media and has had two published by
United Press. "I accept life as it comes, due to my strong
Christian faith. I have had my share of sorrows but life is
too short and I haven't time to fantasise," she remarked. "I
am very down to earth and am content with my friends and
life."

I KNOW HER SO WELL

In a cottage in the valley
the place where I was born.
Lives an old and troubled lady,
Silent memories, all forlorn.

Empty chair beside the fire.
It's been so for many years.
Since the day that he departed,
leaving her with trickling tears.

The joy of living long forgotten,
grief remains there deep within
Reflecting through her failing eyesight,
adoring thoughts maintained of him.

He has gone to far off places,
never again to hold her hand.
She is left in her empty harbour,
clinging to her golden band.

Staring sightless in the firelight
trickling moisture in her eyes.
Sits a sad and lonely woman,
thinking of they're last goodbyes.

Alwyn James, Newtown, Wales

REVELATIONS

Revealing the unknown,
Day by day,
As I peel the orange of life.
'Shock of the new'?
No. just me.
A full stop after every sentence,
Life without an encore.
Funny, I thought,
Could have sworn that was yesteryear.

Lauren Evans, Neath, Wales

WHEN SHADOWS LENGTHEN

When shadows lengthen and the daylight flies
On damask wings to where the sun takes rest,
The dreary night with all its mystic creatures
Swiftly fills the crimson western skies.
Come then, my love, to one who sorely needs you
Guard this pregnant heart
From all those pretty fears that, in you absence,
Thickening night reveals.

For when the cloth of night drops swiftly down
And day's bright robed players take their bows,
When all the stage is hushed, the singers gone
Save for the crystal toned nightingale, who's
Mournful song
Drifts through the limpid air
To where, in warm serenity you stand.
Then my feeble heart forgets its fear of dark
And draws its store of sunshine from your soul.

Valdo Funning, Neath, Wales

TIMES PAST

Oh how I wish I could set the world to rights
And bring back innocence of time
When greed did not rear its ugly head
Yet poverty was shared by everyone.

Then kindness with humility shone through
From neighbours willing to lend a hand
An atmosphere in which we grew
Where man helped out his fellow man.

The sunny Summer days we knew
children being able to play out
Safely after school
Then they'd while away the hours
Making daisy chains in field of flowers

All we had were simple pleasures
Cinema, disco, the beach at leisure
These are to name just a few
That's only if the parent's approved

Strict our upbringing appeared to be
Rules handed down through familys
It was with their best intentions
To bring us up decent honest citizens.

Valerie Thompson, Cwmbran, Wales

A WARNING FOR BOYS

Watch out, watch out, unblemished young boy,
Your unlikely unsuitable friend is coming:
Coming to cast out the innocent thoughts
From behind your widening eyes.

Look out, look out, clean honest young lad
Your grasping untrustworthy friend is coming:
Coming to joyride your car and your girl
Right under your now-confused nose.

Watch it, watch it, bored languid young man,
Your magnetic psychotic friend is coming:
Coming to sully the pure untouched heart
Trapped in your go astray body.

Look now, look now, lost helpless grown man,
Your repulsive blood brother friend is here:
He's trampled and buried your once shining soul,
Cloned himself while you were sleeping.

Karen Watkins, Carmarthen, Wales

THANK YOU LORD

Thank you Lord, for the love that sought and rescued me,
Steadfast love which endures throughout eternity;
Higher love, deeper than my mind can e'er perceive.
Gratefully Your love I receive.

As I sit at Your feet and bask in this great love,
I feel safe and secure and strengthened from above.
Darkness flees and Your peace comes in to fill my heart.
Help me Lord your love to impart.

Meredith Vallis, Pantygasseg, Wales

CLOUDS

Even inside
the busiest of hours
I turn
toward a quiet memory
through a window.
Leaning forward
I reach
for what I can remember
while all around the fading noise
I focus thoughts
on half truths and what ifs
on tastes and smells,
on then
and now I turn
to close my eyes on the light
and hold your smile in my hand
keep it
'til the clouds pass by.

Gareth Wyn Davies, Carmarthen, Wales

SPRINGTIME

Springtime is special to me each year
Memories of lady May so dear
Who loved all the flowers in her garden
Now May rests in the garden of Eden.

Springtime she married the man of her choice
So happy even birds seemed to rejoice
Then to a country hotel by the lake
May was happy for everybody's sake.

In different towns we made our abode
May never complained if rough was the road
Sunshine and storm she said rest for a while
Always it ended with just a sweet smile.

Through wars and depressions she survived
Dealing with trouble before it arrived
Helping the old weak young and hungry
Asking for nothing but to be friendly.

Children came and all went on their own way
May told them when in trouble just to pray
Now her home is in sweet heaven above
Where always there is God's eternal love.

Peter Arthur Butcher, Pontypool, Wales

KING OF THE RING

His punch rained free, quick as the eye
To take his opponent by surprise
Tall handsome man, with his expertise
He could fly like a butterfly, punch with ease
Time after time, his gloves shot out to clout
Find his target, knock his opponent out
People clapped stamped and cheered
A champion boxer, who had no fears
Now retired, he still holds great score
People pray for him, more and more
Admired now for his greatest fight
An ailment, that has taken over his life
He gave his audience, the excitement they craved
Will long be remembered, his smile so brave
His chant of verse's he also made
A memory placed in history's page.

Primrose Matthews, Bedwas, Wales

Born in Abertridwr, **Primrose Matthews** enjoys reading
writing and spending time with her grandchildren. "I start-
ed writing poetry when I retired, to keep my mind active, as
a hobby and to help me make up little stories for my
grandchildren," explained Primrose. "My work is influenced
by people and places of interest and my style is melan-
choly." Aged 65 she is a housewife. She is married to
John and they have five children. "The person I would
most like to meet is Paul Macartney because I like his style
of music so much. My worst nightmare is not being able to
write." Primrose has written many poems and had several
published.

THE LAKE

Oh beautiful lake,
with secrets untold.
mysteries buried
never to unfold.
you have shared romantic dreams,
watched children play.
families have come to view,
day after day.

Oh lake of the deep
the ghosts that you reap
what strange happenings
when all are asleep.
thick fog awaits the night
with the phantoms of the mist
now in sight.

Oh lake of darkness
if only you could reveal
all the things that you have seen.
your knowledge within you will keep
underneath hidden deep.

Carol Rees, Maesteg, Wales

THE BAG

On holiday in Italy, the back row of the bus
Two geordies sat next to us
Everyday was a revelation
Our eyes glued with concentration.
Entrigued? Read on and I'll guarantee
You'll be gobsmacked
With a capital G!

Each day the bag came out
Small and neat, but with loads of clout!
First the flask a gigantic size
next a pillow, what a surprise!

But more was to come, I can assure you
Big bags of crisps and a gameboy too
Camera, binoculars- endless coffee
Sandwiches, fruit and mountains of toffee.
Is all this true? I hear you question
Yes, even tablets for indigestion!

The list could go on - unlike this verse
Oh! I forgot to mention
The essential "Night Nurse"!!

Sandra Lowe, Llanelli, Wales

GLEAMING SEA

Sailing silvered sea
Lighted way from shores lea
Glistening in sylvan light
From the suns might
Sea of sudden calm
Days of gentle balm
Until re-lit by the moons wane
For so long to remain.

Roger Matthews, Penarth, Wales

LIFE THROUGH MY EYES

When I had your letter I didn't know
What quite what to write,
Then I thought of the name of the book
And it made me think!
Do poets think in different ways
So I see the world in different ways
So I always say what I think, feel, see
Or do we hide our true feelings
Behind the words we write? hopeing
That I don't have to face the world,
I think its a gift to make people see
That life is not the same
We all have good times
We all have bad times
We are near enough all the same
According to you I'm blessed with
This gift so I would like you
All to share it with me.

Lorraine West, Bridgend, Wales

RYAN

Under grey hue of twilight star
Ryan friend stands with his guitar
The music is smooth and the beat flows
As he plays for the God he knows
The melody his voice, his only call
Yet he shows his heart through it all
As he looks skyward he believes
So an answer from heaven he receives
A dove flutters down from that land
And nestles snugly into his hand.

Christopher Parks, Swansea, Wales

A COUNTRY STROLL

I like to stroll in summertime
Along the country lanes
Where rain pools like glass mirrors shine
Reflecting their domain.
Like proud tall trees with branches high
And birds perched on the boughs
All sending forth a merry song
And nodding flowers rouse.
Thick bushy hedgerows screen green fields
Where sheep and cattle graze
In leisurely sweet contentment
They while away their days.
Ripe blackberries peep from the hedgerows thick
With leaves of differing hues
And nature's brush with expertise
Did perfect colours choose.
It is a marvellous, wondrous thing
God's blessings seen each day
He guides and leads my faltering steps
Along His righteous way.

Marian Curtis-Jones, Newport, Wales

OUR HOPE

Flash of pink and black, with white feathers blue barred,
Glimpse of jay through dark branched trees,
His raucous warning call shattering the sylvan stillness
As sharp eyes and ears detect unwelcome intruder in his
familiar territory.
Amongst red gold of Autumn's maple and dogwood's orange
and crimson,
Gamekeeper, gun in hand, stalks stealthily across mossy
earth.
Two staccato shots echo over surrounding copse.
Jay drops to ground with lifeless thud,
Small feathers scattering like thistledown over tangled
bushes.

"No more you'll steal my pheasants' chicks and eggs!"

Damp horse chestnut leaves now trodden underfoot
Like discarded tickets lie beneath mortuary of small wood-
land bodies.
Stoats, weasels, hawks, magpies, jays
Nailed by gamekeeper to rough hewn 'vermin rails'
And so, they hang buffeted by wind and weather,
Their once bright fur and feathers now dull and ragged.

Times change, and we with them, wise sages said.
Therefore in their habitat in Britain's woods and fields
May we hope that our protected wild life can always live
In freedom and in peace.

Laura Fost, Llandeilo, Wales

ESCAPE

Feel the warm breeze caressing your cheek
in this land so far from home.
Feet snuggling in to the soft white sand
And feeling free to roam

The sea so blue and green and black,
moves gently in and out,
It's white fingers playing with the shore
listening to the children shout.

We need the sea to travel around
It transports many of our needs.
It's painted by artists in all shapes and sizes
Holds tales of pirates and their deeds.

But it can turn to a whirling frenzy
Toss ships like toys in a bath.
Take the lives of our fishermen
And others in its path.

It is amazing how quickly a boiling sea
Can return to peace and calm
So we can stroll along the shores
And enjoy the sunny balm.

Patricia Newton, Caerphilly, Wales

THE BEAUTY OF LOVE

Love envelopes me and gives me freedom to express
All the wonderful feelings that once were difficult to experi-
ence.
As time moves on emotions get deeper and deeper.
Contentment fills my whole being with an increasing force.
I thank God for my live of lovely expression.
Love has touched me like the brush of a feather.
The security this brings reminds me my composure is
calm.
Fulfilment and happiness go hand in hand.
Marriage was the beginning of a pathway to treasure.
Love has touched me and lightens the load.
It has given me the strength to show
A side of me I longed to feel.
Marriage was the culmination of a dream
Today is the celebration of that dream.

Marjory Price, Abergavenny, Wales

*I would like to dedicate this poem to my husband, Andrew,
who inspired me to write it.*

PAPER (COLOURFUL EXPRESSION)

I looked for paper, inspiration alight,
Meandering imagination, flowing right
Casting shadows as thoughlettes pass me by,
Sweetly lingering, expression harmonised.

Wordlings sensitively scribed,
Pictorially, complete with pride,
The meaning plainly put,
Naked sheets, the unwritten book,

Raped by my words, this page arousal,
Dressed in words of passion,
The alphabetic seeds meaning,
Put it together, to express a feeling,

Sown on this bare sheet are letters,
Grown thoughtfully, to show it matters,
Paper needs the pen not the sword,
To tell the birth of the written word.

If I had not written this verse,
The paper empty of meaning,
But full of possibilities.

Tony Davis, Haverfordwest, Wales

THINK ABOUT IT!

I dreamed one night the sky turned gray-aliens came to
Earth to stay
Spaceships had dropped in every land-for they just couldn't
understand.
When they watched from up above humans living without
love.
They saw us all fight each other-sometimes brother against
brother
They couldn't understand why we-weren't happy in a world
so free
They decided on our Earth to take-every tree and field and
lake
They drove us all into the sea-I saw no boat for you or me.
When I awoke I began to cry-for I didn't want us all to die
If this invasion comes one day-maybe then we'll have to
pay
For we can't even live together-although we're all birds of a
feather
Sometimes its only colour that splits one man from another
Maybe one day we'll choose a shade that's not the one
already made
Sometimes it's the land we live that takes away the love we
give.
A different God for every land-is this the way it was once-
planned
For often it's the God we pray - that parts us at the end of
the day
Can't we use our wits and charms-why must we resort to
arms
When will we agree a voice-that let's us all at last rejoice if
one day my dreams come true-who will take the blame will
you?

Rebecca Rees, Ammanford, Wales

WHAT RIGHT

What right do you have
To take a man's life
What right do you have
To stick in the knife
To take a man from his wife
To take a father from a child
What right do you have
To gloat with all your might
At the sight that you see
What right do you have
To sleep at night
What right do you have
You have no right
Every human being
Deserves basic human respect.

Sonia B West, Treorchy, Wales

LOST LOVE

Alone I stand desolate and forlorn
High on a cliff top, my lost love I mourn.
While far below the mighty sea, crashes to shore
With a thunderous roar.
It's swirling gray waves rushing to and fro,
Why the grief, they what to know?
Harsh stinging rain hides bitter tears,
Why did you leave after so many years?
I hear the sea calling and whispering my name,
Fear not, with me your secret will remain...
Silently the wind carries away my prayer
As into the unknown I step without care.
So do not mourn or grieve for me
For I will be with my lost love, happy and free.

Susan Revell, Peterborough, Cambridgeshire

PARTED ACROSS THE SEA

Your sea is blue
Your sea is green
With sparkling diamonds in between
Your sea is gentle and calm and warm
And looks as it knows not of cruelty or harm.

My sea is harsh and grey and cold
As though it holds secrets never to be told,
It rushes to the shore with angry bent
Then leaves in peace, subdued and spent.
My sea joins yours a world away
To unite as our hearts will,
Please soon be the day.

Patricia Titcomb, Eaton Socon, Cambridgeshire

LOVE LOST

I thought you'd changed
But I find that you are still the same.
Once hurt, I shall restrain
From ever being hurt again.
You said you loved me,
I guess you lied
All those feelings locked up inside.
You showed no emotion and no remorse
Yet you are always willing to use force.
I know we can not exist as one,
For we are like a loaded gun
Forever firing
And without success,
But you must know
I love you no less.

Samantha Potts, Peterborough, Cambridgeshire

TEEN DREAMS

In my dreams I often return to a decade in the past
Back to the 1970's, a mind blowing blast
Days of schoolgirl fantasies tales of a first kiss
Idolising popstars, making a secret wish
Glamrock, platforms, tie-dye flares, yes I had them all
Posters of my favourite band adorned the bedroom wall
Debonair musicians in white satin suits the Rubettes were
their name
Songs of love and tragedy, breaking a girls heart their aim.

At many hectic concert hall I could be seen in the crowd
Feeling faint and dizzy, all churned up inside
Thumping disco music flashing lights above
It is possible to recover from this crazy thing called love
I would close my eyes and make believe I had stole from
them a kiss
Alas everyday reality is never quite this bliss
Did they ever receive my letters
Or open my funny valentine
These thoughts remain for ever with me
And in my mind will always shine.

Maxine Kaye, Peterborough, Cambridgeshire

Dedicated to "The Rubettes" and Alan Williams who has successfully fronted the band for many years with his unique talent.

ON FATHERS DAY

Picture a stern, solemn face.
Toughened skin weathered by years.
Visible portrayal of life's hard lesson
Experienced, not by choice.

Raven black hair, greased back
Away from receding brow.
Piercing blue eyes miss nothing;
No prank, game or guilty look.

Imposing height and breadth.
Frightening when angry,
Secure and comforting
When alone or afraid.

Imagine those same eyes.
Edges crinkled by laughter.
Facial features softened
By love's gentle fingers.

My very own gentle giant
Always strong, unfailingly protective.
Tender heart hidden from the world.
Not from me, miss you Dad.

Karen Davies, Peterborough, Cambridgeshire

A BRIDE IN ROYAL BLUE

"I, Jane, rest from my labour, wrap-up warmly too.
In your loving presence, doted I become, mute,
In my eyes, intensely hot passion glows,
Like blue flame centres of wax candles.
We dabble amongst fields of rye around bumpy cart-tracks.

"I marry you gleefully on ninth of the ninth,
Enwrapped in a lively royal-blue wedding dress,
All mine gracefully upon eighteen sixty nine,
Fits me as great as plumage to a bluebird.
I now feel wholesome in loving adoration.

"Nothing becomes like our romantic honeymoon,
From toil after toil, sowing seeds in muddy fields,
To relaxation in blue-lavender meadows.
I feel submerged in a fine blue deep ocean,
A blue reflected from the infinite sky.

"I handle scented flowers, wild woodland bluebells,
I sip lovely herbal tea from a sapphire urn,
Enjoying my home made blueberry tart.
I have been so far baved in oh, blue.
Kiss me, fumble, even as I sleep neath a tiny ark."

Louis Don Barrow, March, Cambridgeshire

COSMOLOGY

The Big Bang, protons,
Births and deaths of stars.
Black holes and neutrons,
Jupiter and Mars.
The garden of Eden a mystery,
But I understand the allegory.

Scientists in confusion,
Studying the sky.
Came to the conclusion
What's born must surely did.
The forbidden fruit of knowledge bitten,
Revealing how we'll all be smitten!

Omar had a vision,
But no-one paid him heed.
Subjected to much derision,
From his Rubaiyat I quote,
"The first morning of creation wrote
What the last dawn of reckoning shall read."

It is the simpleness of the Great One
That confounds the wisdom of man.

Pamela Willison, West Walton, Cambridgeshire

TOO LATE

The writing was shaky but chosen with care
No words of reproach though he knew they were there
His mind strayed again to the days which were gone
And all he need do was to pick up the phone

"I'm sorry to say" says the voice on the line
Without any warning - a moment in time
He'd rather not hear it confirming his fears
But the voice carries on abusing his ears

"I'm sorry" it says "but we couldn't have known
Or we wouldn't have left him to face it alone"
And his hand feels the tremble that starts in his heart
As he grasps a new meaning to being apart

Just one visit more was his outstanding task
A few minutes even - forgiveness to ask
But the voice is relentless invading his home
And all that he did was to pick up the phone.

Dorothy Blakeman, Peterborough, Cambridgeshire

WILLOW IN A RECTORY GARDEN

I often look at it, held fascinated
By its lofty height, its grotesque twisted shape.
Its old and ugly tangled limbs fight and choke each other
As if bent on systematic pressure.
Down from these limbs trail long skeletal fingers,
Oh, so long and thin; a melancholy drape.

It wears a wooded coat, black, bumpy, pitted,
Stark and forbidding, caked by age-old dust and grime.
I see it and I feel for it growing in this way.
Why so unruly?space to look so violent,
Though sapling once it was virginal and pure,
Just as a child is at birth, untouched by time.

In a rectory garden on a Roman road
Stands this sombre spectre, weeping constantly.
In its image I see a thing in torment.
Is man in his folly reflected in this tree?
It makes me think it is, so it could well be.
Strange this tree grew here, close to a rectory!

Grace Hubbard, St Neots, Cambridgeshire

BENEATH THE MULBERRY TREE

In wintertime we watched the snow
Fall white and cold, then off we'd go
How many snowballs did we throw?
Beneath the mulberry tree.

As spring came round the bluebells grew
The daffodils of yellow, too
Bright colours such a lovely view
Beneath the mulberry tree.

And then came summer, everyday
The sun was warm, below its ray
We filled each hour with fun and play
Beneath the mulberry tree.

With autumn shades of gold and brown
The leaves began to tumble down.
No matter though, we still ran round
Beneath the mulberry tree.

Those years, they quickly passed away
For time moves on, we cannot stay
Oh to go back, just for a day
Beneath the mulberry tree.

Daphne Askew, Wisbech, Cambridgeshire

*Dedicated with love to Mulberry House, my childhood home,
and to Mum, Dad & Janet with whom I shared it.*

DYSLEXIA

They say I'm blind, I cannot see
I'm a little confused, this cannot be.
I can see the world, I see it all
What do they mean, I shout and call.

My peers are cruel, they ridicule and taunt me
I try to stay calm, yet their words still haunt me.
I sit in class and really try to understand
My mum says, "it's ok, just take my hand.

If I am blind, why can I see?
My eyes they work, how can this be?
It's words and numbers that get turned around
They give me no clues, they make no sound.

The word is dyslexia, isn't it strange,
Easy learning is not quite within my range.
I don't read or write very well
I'd like to be happy, but my school life is hell.

Gill Doyle, Sawtry, Cambridgeshire

MY EYES AS POET

see words give birth to simple beauties in life.
I have an appreciation of the wide world
and it throws its own body at me frequently.
But as I sit by this reflecting lake hearing ducks quack
inviting arms connoting love sweep me away.
I am alone as poet
and my eyes separate the tumbling world
which seems to have a bazooka welded to his foot.
The only thing linking the two of us
Is the bird sitting on the fence
and what colour would you say you were?

Rebecca Hankins, Peterborough, Cambridgeshire

KARMA

Each one of us for all we know
Has destiny, a way to go;
And every step along the way
Is predetermined some would say.
Those actions, which have gone before
In pre-existence, I am sure,
Determines what we are today,
The life we live and future way.
And therefore we must tread our path,
Thinking on actions, calming wraith.
Treating kindly and within our power
Lightening the load and improving the hour
Or at the very least, as best we can,
Look kindly on our fellow man.
That we in future time to come
After this span, this life is done
May in a future, some distant day,
Return renewed to find our way.

Jean Regan, Peterborough, Cambridgeshire

THE PRICE OF LOVE

If you should die,
the scream I would scream would be so loud, that no one
but I would hear it, as it would be contained within my
being, as if I too had been struck by the arrow of death
straight to my heart.

I would feel nothing, see nothing, for the world outside
would fail to enter my empty space of grief.

I know that my heart, soul, and life itself, would be soon to
follow yours,
As we have been of one soul and one love for too long to be
separated by death.

Joyce B Burton, Peterborough, Cambridgeshire

REASONING

When a child is beaten and left scarred of face, I have to
wonder about this human race.
When an old man is murder for the sake of some pence, I
have to question those lawyers in defence.
When thousands of people die from needing aid, I have to
live with my pennies never paid.
When the innocent are slaughter for the sake of taking
time, I can't comprehend why giving just a mime.
When across the world every day many more poor people
painfully die, I just can't, understand why.

They say it is the devils work, that in each of us dose lurk.
But I can't help thinking that there is no god and we are
not lead, that if 'he' were true there would be no bloodshed.
And I can't help but notice it would be the almighty's vice,
that he turns the cheek while we pay the price.

Rebecca Glenn, Peterborough, Cambridgeshire

LOVE'S SONNET

Singing, dancing, bursting with happiness-my heart does all this
Whilst a star shoots across the sky, smiling and throwing me a kiss
One swelling, bountiful moon grins as I tell him my wish
It can't fail to come true on a night like this!
Water lilies, suspended as precious pearls dancing in the liquid night
Rippling and sparkling under my new friend's fairy tale light
What have I done so well to see such a sight?
For nothing could compare to the feelings I have on this night!
Secrets wait to be spilled urged on by eager star shine
Protected by my heart for now, my secrets remain mine
Enchanted night! You already know, but will learn more in time
For on such a night, he will look to the moon and see my dream shine...
I will wait in my paradise for his inevitable kiss
I will wait forever for another night like this.

Jane Besser, March, Cambridgeshire

A YOUTH REMEMBERED

How old I feel in my grey-haired nook,
With shuffling feet and dog-eared book.
The velveteen curtains focus gloom
Through to the heart of my drawing room.

But I can remember the sunshine
Shine on novels never read or seen,
Painting the living room in blue and gold;
I can remember not being old,
And stumbling over some new word,
Hearing music I had never heard,
Feeling a face with a sheen like silk,
Seeing a shoulder like freckled milk.

But I am blind, and my wrinkled brain
Is such an imperfect window pane.
Yet I know, the sun is a transient flare
And the world itself but a troubled fly;
So why should the lord of the universe care
For the senseless tear in a blind man's eye?

George Payne, March, Cambridgeshire

A PICTURE OF THE ARTIST

And whilst you paint your canvas dreams
With pastel shades of mauve and blue,
Plan brighter style, for in a while
You'll gain the love that waits you,
And dreams,
From canvas will come true

Artistic pictures describe the scenes
Defined by dark cerebral thoughts,
And from your mind, all hopes defined,
Will move from profane sanctums fraught
With fears;
Into the safety of your court.

So choose the shades you use with care
Paint scenes, content on canvas clear,
Your pictures then, will show you when;
Sometime when dreams are never near;
They will,
One day, on your portraits appear.

Dave Stevens, March, Cambridgeshire

DIARY OF A STABLE CAT

Here I lay in the old wooden barn
Prowling my way all around the farm
I sleep in the warm fresh stable hay
Catching the mice that pass each day
I am the only cat on the yard
Keeping the mice away at times is hard
In summer I like to lie in the sun
But winter is not very fun
People come from far and wide
To be taught how to ride
These great big horses carry them all
Then they have a rest in their stall
The horses then eat their oats
While riders brush their golden coats
When it rains I stay inside
And in the hay is where I hide
This is how I spend my day
Sleeping amongst the warm fresh hay.

Becky Fowler, Guyhirn, Cambridgeshire

Becky Fowler said: "I first became interested in poetry
about three years ago when I was at school. I had my first
poem published about a year ago. I mostly write poetry
about animals. I like the works of Betjeman and D H
Lawrence of which I have a first edition of his poetry collec-
tion. I am a 17-year-old kennel assistant at my local
boarding kennels, which helps give me ideas for my poetry.
My aim is to have a book of my poems published. I enjoy
reading, writing, autograph collecting and horseriding. I
attended Guyhirn Primary and Neale Wade Community
College."

HOLLOW WORDS

The blind lady sits at the end of the day
Watching children play out their dreams:
Doctors and nurses, diseases and curses.
Reality's not what it seems.

As her only mother faded from her sight
Memories stayed to fill the space;
Framed by her smiling, her loving beguiling,
But no rhyme matched her perfect face.

At school she experienced education-
Shadows, her only playground friends:
Nudging and winking at her frantic blinking.
Verses she'd never comprehend.

For her there were no Valentines from lovers;
Only unknown hands led the way-
No-one to write to; to touch and give sight to.
Meaningless phrases came to stay.

Now the blind lady's name is engraved in stone
Words were candles in her darkness
And wouldn't you know it-she was a poet.
Songs of glory for the heartless.

Mark Rasdall, Ely, Cambridgeshire

REACH FOR THE MOON

Come with me into a fantasy world,
You'll be amazed at what you'll learn.
Forget your problems past and present
And dream of the fulfillment's that you yearn.

Reach into a magical bottomless pool
Of activities only you can achieve.
Release your innermost fears
And trust, hope, have faith and believe.

Believe in yourself, dispel all your doubt
It will hinder your progress no end
Reach for the stars and the moon if you dare
Soon your enemy will be your friend.

Susan Cooper, Great Yarmouth, Norfolk

JOG YOUR MEMORY

Do not dwell on memories that fill the eyes with tears...
As your mind goes wandering along the path of years.
Try to recollect the days of joy and happiness-
Not the sad experiences that darken and depress.
When life seems blank and you are tempted to give way
Just you jog your memory... Why? only yesterday
Some hidden flash of beauty made you pause and catch
you breath.
You wondered at the mystery of life and birth and death.
You felt a thrill of gratitude for friendship fond and true,
You lifted up your weary eyes and saw a wider view.
You do not have to think a long way back before you find
A lot of good and lovely things stored up inside the mind.
Blessing to be thankful for, look round and you will see
When you're sorry for yourself just jog your memory.

Alice M Reynolds, Mattishall, Dereham, Norfolk

REMEMBERING WHEN

He walks along the beach and remembers,
Twenty years ago, when he was ten years old.
The summer hours they seemed unending.
Happy sunny days, did it ever rain?
Digging, scooping trenches in the sand,
The in coming tide would fill then flood them.
And when the waves washed back to sea,
Toffee coloured pebbles and shells glistened in the sun.
Seaweed trails in many shades of green,
To pop and squeeze, or decorate a sand castle.
And when the tide went out, rock pools to investigate,
Baby crabs, starfish and waving flower-like sea anemones.
Picnic food a little gritty, drinks a little warm,
And always the gulls, hovering hopefully by.
His secret wish to return, to live and work here.

Now standing at the waters edge,
On thick polluted oil-slicked sand,
Gently holding a blackened lifeless sea brids,
What silent grief, to witness the dying of this place he
loves.
This must not, cannot be price of progress!

Cynthia King, Diss, Norfolk

THE BEACH

The sea is a ripple in a bath of blue paint,
The clouds are rolls of cotton wool floating in the peace of
eternity,
The sand is a field of golden corn surrounded by soft
breaths of fresh air,
The pebbles and rocks are mountains dotted around a
world of chatting humans,
The gentle breeze is a gust of fresh air exhaled around the
world,
The sun is a yellow beach ball floating in an exotic pale
blue sea.

Candi Baxter, Kings Lynn, Norfolk

WIZARDRY DO

I'm wizardry diddery do
I tell children what to do
I fly through the air
Without a care
Co's I'm wizardry diddery do
Stirring my hubbly bubbly stew
The things I find
When flying around
I put in my bubbly stew
I'm wizadry diddery do
Now I've finishes my bubbly stew
To fly on my broom
Under the moon
So now I'll be watching you
Co's I'm
Wizardry diddery do.

Glenda Rowbottom, Great Yarmouth, Norfolk

A TOKEN OF LOVE

In a drawer I found her ring,
Just a plain and simple thing,
No sparkling stones - a plain white band,
But history lay in my hand.

In days gone by he'd left his wife,
He fought to make a better life,
So far away in foreign land,
He then had made this plain white band.

He kept it safe through blood and pain,
Not knowing if they'd meet again.
With battle done they brought him home,
Broken, and no more to roam.

For her man she did her best,
And when she laid him down to rest
She knew, though long they'd been apart,
He held her always in his heart.

When her time came she passed away,
And left the ring I wear today,
A memory to light my life,
Of Grandad and his precious wife.

Alice Ackland, Kings Lynn, Norfolk

THE END

Harmonies played to awaken him
And the wisping mist came to carry him,
So he opened up the light from his heart
Dispersing the darkness from around him
And he was finally released.
The weight of his pain was lifted away
His long suffering has at last ceased
And he was now pure and free,
And forever to be at peace.

Andrew Parker, Melton Constable, Norfolk

Andrew Parker said: "What happens after we die? Who knows, but you would hope that for someone who had been suffering for a long time that death would be a release - a chance, after all the suffering and waiting to finally get some sleep."

JANUARY ROSE

After the floods, black ice and snow,
I venture on to my patio,
And look about in great dismay,
My plants and shrubs have been swept away.
But wait, a small pink bud I see,
Clinging to a broken tree,
This little flower, has fought for life,
So I cut it free, with my garden knife.
The petals are soft, the scent is sweet,
To find this is a New Year's treat.
I bring the rose into the warm,
It will escape the coming storm.
The lovely flower brings me a sign,
That the year ahead will turn out fine.

Diane Berthelot, North Walsham, Norfolk

LOVE

How little we learn from the lesson of life,
How much we would reap if we heeded our strife.
How little we need if we did but know,
How much we would gain if our feelings we'd show.
How much we could give if we were not greedy.
How much better we'd feel if we helped the needy.
How we could change the world and it's sorrow,
By starting today that others may follow.
Little by little the love would enforce,
The longing of man to go back home to his source.

Sylvia Davies, Norwich, Norfolk

ONE SUMMERS NIGHT

I had to leave for some fresh air.
The coffee house seemed too claustrophobic.
My emotions pushed me out of the crowded room
Where empty tables lay waiting.

The warm breeze refreshed me, my glowing cheeks did cool,
And I heard the soft romantic music fade away into the
night.
Dancing surf washed away then reached again,
Sea gulls silhouetted against the setting sun.
The silver ocean beckoned,
Its coastline stretching for centuries.
The dunes a mountainous terrain of fun and sand.

For that sweet night was the one that changed your life,
And you joined me.
We danced beneath the stars
With an extra pair of feet between us
That slept through your beautiful smile.

Anna Whitley, Norwich, Norfolk

PURGATORY

A sexual cauldron of sin,
That place that exists within,
Invading me as I sat,
Forging a reality so flat,
Forbidden desires refuse to disappear,
Why can't my choice be more clear,
Hell is an existence I know to be true,
It comes and goes leaving me black and blue,
Tormented is my body and soul,
Burning a passage to leave my role,
Condemned am I,
Condemned I shall remain,
Never the same again,
The flesh I will have no more,
Blood from my wrists start to pour,
I shall end my life,
Damning everything in a catatonic plight.

David Fairchild, Norwich, Norfolk

DEDICATED TO THOSE WITH ALZHEIMERS

Hello, do I know you? What's your name?
That's a nice name. Have we met before?
Do I know you?

I like your face. You've got a nice face
My cousin's laughing, he says we all met last week, I forget
sometimes
Do I know you?

What's your name then? That's a nice name.
My brother knows someone by that name
I've seen you before, haven't I? I get a bit confused some-
times
Do I know you?

Oh, it's time for us to go, I've had a lovely day
It's been nice meeting you again
I think I know you, I forget your name.
Do I know you?

Henry William Mobbs, Norwich, Norfolk

SEEING FORM WITHIN

An angel has a vision,
A vision to free her tangled mind,
She stops in the crowded street,
And closes her once pure eyes.

The noise in the distance is destroyed
By people rushing and shouting,
These are then all blurred together,
Destroying the distinguished, all features are lost.

Now all that is left is natural force,
The gentle wind across her glistening face,
Soon that is gone and only a heartbeat remains,
One which cannot be conquered.

Now that the angels mind is cleansed and free
She sees a vision from her soul,
Now she is free to open her eyes
And view the new beauty from within.

Chris Belcher, Norwich, Norfolk

SPRING-TIME IN COSTESSEY

Spring-what can I say? the beauty of it all
Takes my breath away.
The colours of the flowers
Rainbow hues, green and gold.
Beauty of the blossom, as we watch the buds unfold.
Hedges with the nest of birds
Tucked among the branches.
By the stream, enhances.
Birds sing sweetly as they search
The titbits for their young.
Trees sway by the river reflected by the sun
Children playing on the bridge
With sunlight in their hair
What joy to be in tender years,
To be as fresh as air
It's spring-time here in Costessey
What a lovely place to live.
Who needs exotic places
With all that Costessey has to give.

Muriel Roe, Norwich, Norfolk

ORB

In the ink of space
Spins an orb
Of many a face.
Sapphire blue
And emerald green
All the beauty
That's ever been.
Within her core
Beats hope and life
Chasing out
Tearful strife.
And she spins
Throughout the years
Casting a torch
Upon our fears.
As the sun breaks the day
And the moon crowns the night
The centuries pass
Through eternal light.

Victoria Ellen Painting, Sudbury, Suffolk

Born in Havering in Essex **Victoria Painting** enjoys reading, art, music, the outdoors, travelling and writing. "I started writing poetry when I was a little girl but wrote my first set of poems when I was 13," she remarked. "I write because I enjoy it. It gives me great pleasure. My work is influenced by people, landscapes emotions, news and music and my style is contemporary but very varied. I would say I'm experimental. I would like to be remembered in the hearts and minds of those who love and respect me." Aged 18 she is an undergraduate student with an ambition to live and work in America but mainly to travel the world, meet new people and see the things she has only dreamed about. Victoria has written many poems and had several published.

LOST

At the centre of my heart I found
A deep, dark hole,
An emptiness
A cavern
A deep embittered soul.

At the centre of my heart I need
A love to make me whole,
A friend,
A companion,
Someone to mend my soul.

Sophie Johnson, Haverhill, Suffolk

MY LITTLE WOMAN

You came to me life the gift of sight
To someone who doesn't always see the light
The day you were born, you brightened my day
Like morning dew and long summer days,
You had tiny hands and feet to match
I held you so close, you seemed to smile back.
From that day on and each day past
You grow more and more, your growing fast.
First you sit then you crawl
till one day you wont need me at all.
When the day comes for you to leave my nest.
And take on the world and do your best
One thing will remain true.
As from the day you were born till the day Ill have to leave
you.
Taht no matter how near or far you are from me,
I'll be there for you should you ever need me.

Belinda Allen, Mendlesham, Suffolk

EMOTIONS

She sits by the window, her painful thoughts far away
She's not thinking of the future, but long lost days
Her old eyes are sad, as she thinks about her love
Gone so long ago, out of reach up above,
Her memories flood back into her weary head
Her slowly beating heart, is with the dead.
The young boy she'd loved for so long and so true
Loving sweethearts for so many years through
From childhood to manhood, always them two.
Now life has torn them apart, she knows not what to do
How can she go on?
Now that he has gone?
The years just pass her by.
The time is seems to fly
She sits and waits for his gently call
And then deep in his arms she will fall
There is nothing else she needs or wants to do.
Except my darling to be forever with you.

Janet Borrett, Bury St Edmunds, Suffolk

TRUST

The trust which once wrung true like well cast bells
Is cracked and now must be recast.
The sonorous dell no longer rings true clear.
Which way shall this peal ring out now
And claim another day of thought?

The truth, which ever clear in mind to feel,
Is no more close to each visage front.
The face has scars and lines to show.
Which side shall point this honest man
And hide the secrets in once taught thoughts?

Sacred Heart..

David Ross, Ipswich, Suffolk

AFTERWARDS

There are places where I'll never walk again
Some music I shall never want to hear
And flowers whose scented petals I shall leave unplucked
Because their piercing fragrance brings you near

Days will drift like leaves over the time we shared
Gently obscuring happiness and pain
Sunrise to moon-set weaving webs of hours
To hide what is past and wont return again

But sometimes unbidden memory does stir
At some familiar perfume, sound or scene
Then looking back with infinite regret
I weep for everything that might have been.

Megan Samuel, Stowmarket, Suffolk

IN OUR FORTIES

We now need to change tables in restaurants for fear of a chill
But there are definitely more draughts that there used to be.

Reading glasses are needed for newspapers, timetables and covers of CDs
But the print is definitely smaller than it used to be.

Pardon is a much familiar word and lots of conversations have to be repeated.
But you definitely talk quieter than you used to, and background noises are much louder.

Stairs are steeper
High heels higher
Distances longer
Night clubs open, and close, later
Birthdays come round more quickly.

Can't wait for our fifties.

Christine Laverock, Woodbridge, Suffolk

LETTER FROM AN INJURED LOVE

If ever you come to find this letter,
I fear that I may be no more,
a tender kiss seals these words I write,
at this treacherous time of war.

Please tell our children what happened to me,
make them believe what I did was right,
do not be afraid I will watch from above,
A guiding hand when you fear the night.

The love we have I will carry always,
still burning so bright in this dying heart,
I will never forget the time that we had,
your touch lingers on as I sadly depart.

Suzy Boon, Felixstowe, Suffolk

IRISH SUMMER

A summer magic lies upon the land.
A blessed lull before the Winter's storm.
The patient cattle dreaming stand
And only Butterflies and Bees have life.

The Donkey dozes in his shafts,
His master drowsy, nods upon his way
As if a faery potion they had drunk
Bestowing slumber on them where they lay.

But yet must man and plodding beast unite
To gather in the precious golden grain
To cut the turf to keep the fire bright
And keep out want and Winter's rain.

Patricia Cox, Ipswich, Suffolk

A WHISPER OF SILENCE

Listen for a whisper,
Feel a soft breath against your face.
Touch the warm breeze that blows behind you.
She's there saying "I love you",
Which ever path you take.

She is in the sunrays above,
In the rainbow, that holds your memories
Her teardrops.
The rain beating against your breast.

She is the snowflake that falls silently,
The moons silver crest.
Her spirit will surround you
In many earthly forms until

You are called together
Upon your departing morn
"Just listen, for that whisper."

Lizzy Usher, Woodbridge, Suffolk

THE COMING OF THE SNOW

I feel the coming of the snow
And soon twill be time to go.
This is the Winter of my season.
Pain and ancient bones the reason.
Black winged harpies a vigil keep
In deepest night disturb my sleep
Will you be sad to see me go?
For soon the coming of the snow.

Dark days of winter now are sent.
All fruits are picked the harvest spent.
Grim reaper dons a cloak of black.
Picks up his scythe and gathering sack
Dead friends in laboured dreams I find
Patient grey figures, in frozen mould
Loved still, their blood long since cold
Grieve not now, for I must go
Wait its the coming of the snow.

Good and ill my years have past
Some spark of light I hope will last
Leave some love regretted hate!
For all I took that crossed my plate.
My light remember if you will
Forgive the bad, forget the ill!
Be not sad for its time to go
Welcome the coming of the snow.

Peter Davey, Ipswich, Suffolk

LINNET'S LANE

Stay, look and listen, tread softly, ghosts abide here
In the ground and all around in Linnet's Lane.
Here before saxon, then roman legion marching to
Colchester,
Children of history played in marsh meadows leading to
Stourmere, where wild fowl linger still.
Dawn mists draw vapour figures in hedgerows by the river
Where servants paused drawing water for the villa itself
Now a phantom.
Where do they lie now, those of yesteryear?
Be still, canst thou not feel, earthly shells, still here below,
In the cold earth, safe even from the ploughmans share.
Ghosts sharing earlier spirits even of flint knappers,
Tailored in skin of strange creatures,
Once native here, long gone away.
A grudging soil, beaten by wind and rain, offers up
To keenest eye, long lost belemnite and devils toenail
Time's gifts, mocking still, mortals transience.
Stay, look and listen, tread softly,
All of time is around you, here
In linnet's lane.

James Allen, Haverhill, Suffolk

GOODBYE JUDO

I knelt with breaking heart, this was when we had to part
With us for so many years, now divided, wet with tears
He left us in seconds, a lovelier doggy world beckons
Memories so sharp and clear even now after a year
Not a day we dont speak of our friend, faithful, loving to
the end
He will stay within each heart so in one way we'll never
part
He lies beneath a rambling rose, with his ball just by his
nose.

Bryony, Ipswich, Suffolk

YOUNG LOVE

You helped me mature
by your knowledge and science
and male view of life.
If at times love brought passion
that was natural and nobler by far
than cold calculated reason
try though I might
to see life through your eyes
I could not be else
but a woman.

From our times together
and ways far apart
we loosed gently the ties
that once bound us
and savoured some moments
for eternity.

Aline Longman, St Edmunds, Suffolk

WE NEVER SEEM TO BE ALONE

We never seem to be alone
It really is quite sickening;
You're always on the telephone.

I want to get you on you own,
My pulse is madly quickening;
We never seem to be alone.

You always help, you never moan,
When someone else needs counselling
You're always on the telephone.

To interruptions we are prone,
I only wish to me you'd cling;
We never seem to be alone.

Our friendship's in the danger zone,
The warning light is flickering;
You're always on the telephone.

Before I face the great unknown
I'm longing for a final fling;
We never seem to be alone,
You're always on the telephone.

Grahame Godsmark, Walberswick, Suffolk

SUFFOLK I

The lovely morning sky
The sun beams down with such delight upon the gathered
fields

As day rolls by the shadows ply and linger in the breeze
And you can hear the whisper of wind up in the trees

As sun peeps through a cloudy sky the farmer seeks his
task
To gather in the bales of straw to help the winter last

Night falls so slowly the gentle shadows gone
There's the coolness of the evening, birds have lost their
song

But at the end of the day a red sky at night
Gives us the feeling that tomorrow will be all right

The fields of gold are here again
But the fields of gold will go

For they reap them with the harvester
And when they reap them then they sow

The sun gleams down this day oh! will the morning last
If the sun gleams down will it last the whole day through

They talk of rain coming again
To mositen the harvest field but may it stay away for
another
day for enoughs enough they say.

                    Dennis Theobald, St Edmunds, Suffolk

GOOD FRIDAY

On this grey day
from the window of my car
iridescent hues on broken wing
hold the gaze.
The momentarily empty road
stretching to infinity
defeats the dying bird.
She huddles down
gently
as if brooding a clutch of new lives.

As blood-red light gives way to green
All time is held
in her clouding eye.
For an infinitesimal moment
we share the knowledge of death.
Then it passes
and her small, still greyness lies
bare of dignity.

And I remember another death,
a Friday acceptance,
a Dove brooding over the earth.

Sylvia Eden, Lavenham, Suffolk

WITH INNER EYES

The eye of a poet sees wonderful things,
A rainbow in a dragonfly's wings.
Diamonds in a waterfall,
Or an angel's song in a lark's call.

The cornfield ripples in the breeze
Like restless waves upon the seas.
The music in a blackbird's song
That fills the air the whole day long.

The beauty of our world abounds,
The things we see - the lovely sounds.
We know the power of a mother's sigh
And hear the joy of a baby's cry.

The moonlight path across the lake
Where gently glides a duck and drake.
The flowers, like children, dance and nod
In places where the Saints have trod.

Elizabeth Davies, Rickinghall, Suffolk

REFLECTIONS

True love is a rare quality
Seldom achieved in a lifetime.
Yet a meeting of kindred souls
Who have the same visions
And the same perceptions
Is a wondrous gift.
Meetings may be short
But the dye is cast.
Life will never be the same;
The longing to share one's thoughts,
The touch of a hand,
A gentle kiss....
Perhaps we will meet
In another life.
Better to remain a loner,
To dream, perhaps,
Of what life could be
In another age - another time....

Helen Persse, Woodbridge, Suffolk

Helen Persse daughter of a dramatist/author said: "I have
always had a love of words and much intuition, but as a
single parent of three children and a teacher of dyslexics
and others I didn't have much time for writing until about
two years ago, when I had a sudden right-sided stroke,
affecting my limbs but not my brain; giving me time to
catch up with my literary work. I have had about nine
poems published within the last six months and have an
anthology of my poems due to be published in due course."

WHERE'S MUM?

Steven's Mum has gone away,
If his Dad knows why, he doesn't say.
Steven lives with his Dad and brother, Ben,
He's only six, and Ben's just ten.

Today, at school, they'd made Mother's Day cards.
Mrs Bryce had really tried very hard
To ensure that Steven wasn't upset
And he hadn't cried - at least, not yet.

"Will you make a card for a special day?
"Perhaps for Grandma, or Aunty Kay?"
"Can I do one for my Dad instead?"
Mrs Bryce smiled and nodded her head.

To Steven this whole thing didn't make sense.
He went out to his Dad, who was mending the fence.
"We made cards today, Dad and I did two,
"One for Grandma, and one for you."

Dad put down his tools to give him a hug,
(He almost knocked over his coffee mug!)
"It'll be alright, son, just wait and you'll see."
"I think you're the best Dad there ever could be!"

Sue Smith, Felixstowe, Suffolk

SHATTERED EMOTIONS

A glass lays shattered on the floor
Close to where I stand
I felt no pain although I saw
The blood upon my hand

I felt nothing, I was completely numb
My limbs had lost their will
Emotions died, tears wouldn't come
And time was standing still

How long I stood, I just don't know
The blood formed a darkened pool
I didn't try to stem the flow
Just stood there like a fool

I read again the note you left
The words tumbled in my head
You've gone away, my soul's bereft
I wish that I was dead

I'll buy a glass and remove the stain
My body will survive
But first I have to feel some pain
To prove my heart's alive

Jackie Johnson, Needham Market, Suffolk

GIFTED

He wished for the power of speech,
Yet his thoughts behold such wondrous language

He longed for the strength to run,
Yet he always enters my mind at great speed.

He yearned for the freedom of flight,
Yet I saw him fly higher than many others.

He was not blessed with the things he wanted,
Yet he has such a strong ability-
He is gifted with the ability to love.

Caryn Squires, Lowestoft, Suffolk

DOING THE HOUSEWORK

Writing poetry, and doing the housework.
Both evoke the same responses.
You know it has to be done, and it sits, waiting
Building up, becoming more urgent
Then one day, it refuses to be ignored and
You launch yourself into a full scale attack
Delving into recesses, shaking out the dust,
Unearthing things long forgotten and long unused
A mad frenzy of cleansing and purging
Always doing more than you meant to
And ending, feeling drained but satisfied.
Then you realise your work will be seen
Will it stand up to scrutiny?
The trick is, that no-one else knows
About the mould behind the dresser,
Or the dust swept under the carpet.

Julie Ashton, Ipswich, Suffolk

DICENTRA SPECTABILIS

Cancer was your father and your mother
and the disastrous gift they bestowed on you
for surviving their fractured union.

You were never more truly your father's son
then the moment your heritage of suffering
finally bore such dreadful fruit.

You were the pain-racked heir to a realm of torment
where fear was unleashed and stalked the land.

You entered your kingdom of pain and took up your
sceptre and orb,
Ascending your throne as your long bones crumbled inside
you.

Sarah Jondorf, Newmarket, Suffolk

A SEAT FOR HISTORY

The other day
Your existence was took away
Nevertheless you will live on.

It seemed unjustifiable
Why you had to die
Only memories remain.

Emotional people
Remembering a person
Who cared so much.

Your face, your voice
Will haunt me
Until the heartache eases.

Life can be so cruel
Now there is to be an additional
Family vacant chair.

Andrea Grimes, Newmarket, Suffolk

MOON OF DREAMS

Crisp and clear, moonlit sky of this night,
Bathing our world with such gentle light.
Soft shades of silver and blue within.
Cotton bud clouds weave serenely by,
Dappling white, this midnight blue sky.
Caressing cool breeze I feel on my face.
Standing beneath this scene entrancing,
Dreams and wishes of my heart are dancing,
Held fast within this moment so fair.
Whilst this vision holds my wistful gaze
The clouds are clearing, in their wake a haze
Vibrant, beautiful - gently forming
Colours! This midnight sky adorning.
My breath holds fast - oh! the beauty there!
Indigo, violet, green, pink, gold.
An awesome sight I now behold
A perfect rainbow encircles the moon!
My soul is moved, something stirs from within,
I hear a voice murmur - of all your dreams begin
Now make reality of them.

Sally Jane Barnes, Woodbridge, Suffolk

THE ILLEGITIMATE

The illegitimate child he stood alone
Deserted by family with heart of stone
Two strangers they did take him in
And saved him from the refuge bin
Nursed him with tender love and care
Cradled him on their lap sat upon a chair
Fed clothed and loved him as if he was their own
Even deprived themselves with not a single moan
The years passed by and the child did thrive
For it was no surprise the boy would survive
He had a will of his own and was strong of mind
Yet underneath he had a nature ever so kind
He went to school and was taught a trade
Having an agile mind as sharp as a blade
He travelled the world by going to sea
And those he met he left his memory
But his world fell apart on that December day
When his Mums turn came to join God's way
His life now became like an empty street
As each year passes by brings its tearful greet.

Harold Stephenson, Kircubbin, County Down

REFLECTIONS ON THE RIVER

Reflect how the water, like life, flows by,
emerging from a swampy tarn or spring,
where shyly in grass it plays,
hiding and seeking to tantalise the eye,
kaliderscoping colours which then bring
such wanderlust to our bopeeping days.

The stream at its head is destiny led
to increase in size, to dazzle the eyes,
to shoot down the falls where gravity calls
to the river that lies increasing in size.
The basin is bed, then off to be wed
No longer crawls, no longer stalls.

The river meets the sea as is the norm
evaporating in the shining sun
to join the sky and reborn as rain.
Energy, matter, simply changes form
like the river. When our day is done,
if we come back what will we be again?

Peter Huggins, Raglan, Wales

MERMAID

When the rushing winds at night
Roar through the trees my heart is woken
With painful joy. The raging storm
The voice of a distant queen has spoken,
Snatched from off the ringing shore.
Like salty spray the drops of rain
Come flying through the starless skies
To lash upon the window pain.
And all at once I feel the sea
Running back into my veins,
With icy throb am claimed once more
By hopeless hope and watery chains.
Through the woodlands, wild and free,
I sense it salting up the streams,
Slipping over sluggish sod,
Thundering into hidden seams.
Over sand and over stones,
From far across the blackened fields,
Into flesh and very bones,
The night a heaving ocean yields.

Andria J Cooke, Norwich, Norfolk